I SPEAK ENGLISH

A GUIDE TO TEACHING ENGLISH
TO SPEAKERS OF OTHER LANGUAGES—
LISTENING, SPEAKING, READING, WRITING

by
Ruth Johnson Colvin

LITERACY VOLUNTEERS OF AMERICA, INC.

All proceeds from the publication of this book go to further the work
of Literacy Volunteers of America, Inc.

ABOUT LITERACY VOLUNTEERS OF AMERICA, INC.

Literacy Volunteers of America, Inc. (LVA) is a national, nonprofit, educational organization founded in Syracuse, New York, by Ruth Colvin in 1962. LVA provides materials and services to assist in the development of volunteer tutorial programs in Basic Literacy (BL) and English for Speakers of Other Languages (ESOL) for adults and teens throughout the United States and Canada. Professional and volunteer staff members are trained to manage local programs. Tutors assist adults and teens to read, write, understand, and speak English. LVA has an active network of state organizations and midlevel systems to support its almost 400 affiliated programs. Extending beyond its affiliates, LVA's training materials and related services are used by organizations and programs in libraries, churches, correctional facilities, adult basic education and public school classes, colleges, and universities. Since its founding, LVA has stressed learner-centered instruction and the use of real-world materials to promote literacy and English language acquisition.

Literacy Volunteers of America, Inc.

635 James Street
Syracuse, New York 13203 USA
Phone: 1-800-582-8812
Fax: 315-472-0002

99B10016

ISBN-0-930713-90-7
LVA Order #91052

PROJECT COORDINATOR AND PRODUCTION EDITOR: GEORGE DEMETRION
COPY EDITORS: SUSAN JAMES AND BARBARA SCHLOSS
DESIGN: DEBORAH A. DiROMA, CREATIVE FX

ABOUT THE AUTHOR

RUTH JOHNSON COLVIN, Founder of LVA

Ruth Colvin is the founder and served as first president of Literacy Volunteers of America, Inc. (LVA). At present she sits on the Curriculum and Field Services Committee of LVA and is a lifetime member of the Board of Directors. She continues to be active as a volunteer tutor in both Basic Literacy (BL) and English for Speakers of Other Languages (ESOL), adapting new methods and approaches to continuously improve upon LVA's model of one-to-one and small group tutoring.

Since 1962, when Mrs. Colvin started LVA, she and her husband, Bob, have traveled all over the United States and the world giving BL and ESOL workshops. The recipient of seven honorary Doctorate of Humane Letters degrees, Mrs. Colvin was awarded the United States of America's President's Volunteer Action Award, the nation's highest award given to a volunteer in 1987. She was inducted into the National Women's Hall of Fame in 1993.

Mrs. Colvin is also author or coauthor of:

TUTOR: A Collaborative Approach to Literacy Instruction, a handbook focusing on learner-centered adult literacy instruction

READ, an assessment tool to use for adult new readers

A Way with Words: The Story of Literacy Volunteers of America

Great Traveling After 55, a "how to" book for veteran travelers as well as new ones

In the Beginning Was the Word: Teaching Reading and Writing Through the Bible, a handbook to use with students who want to read the Bible

ACKNOWLEDGMENTS

I gratefully acknowledge the help given to me over the past 20+ years by tutors, students, professionals, and volunteers in the field of Teaching English to Speakers of Other Languages (TESOL). This book blends and incorporates the most practical ideas for effective tutoring that I have learned from interviews with practitioners and students; from workshops, training, and classes; from professional journals, reports, and books; and from my own experience.

This book does not claim that the techniques and principles suggested are original. I am indebted to a number of authors whose writings have reaffirmed my own convictions or whose creative ideas I have adapted. Thousands of students and tutors who have participated in LVA training have also contributed to this fourth edition of *I Speak English* by adding their ideas and sharing their experiences. I am grateful for what they have taught me. While the book does cover some theory, the emphasis is on the practical and effective lessons that work in real-life situations.

Visits to schools where English is taught to speakers of other languages—both in the United States and elsewhere—have sensitized me to other cultures, traditions, and languages, as well to the desire of so many students to be able to communicate effectively in English.

In this fourth edition, I have drawn extensively from the insights of ESOL specialists to incorporate the Communicative Language Teaching Approach, which emphasizes practical language use, comprehension, and the integration of all four skills—listening, speaking, reading, and writing. I want to thank the many individuals who have helped by sharing their talents and time in the preparation of earlier editions of this book. Special thanks to these dedicated reviewers—Susan Bury, Judy Cheatham, Elissa Director, Kevin Freer, Virginia Gilbertson, Pierre Mali, Teri McLean, Joan Morley, Tom Mueller, Andrea Nash, Pat Peterson, David Red, Evey Renner, Nancy Ryder, and Kim Hughes Wilhelm—and to my editors, George Demetrion and Joye Shaffer, whose comments and suggestions have also contributed to this fourth edition. My deep appreciation goes to Jodi Crandall, LVA's ESOL Consultant, who not only reviewed earlier drafts but also the final one. And thanks, too, to the many students and tutors who have provided me with some of the rich examples and case histories included in this book.

RJC
Syracuse, New York
August 29, 1997

The Publication of the 4th Edition of *I Speak English* was made possible by the Lewis Trinity Fund, Central New York Community Foundation.

CONTENTS

Literacy Volunteers of America, Inc.

CONTENTS - (con't.)

Literacy Volunteers of America, Inc.

CONTENTS - (con't.)

I dedicate this book to all those who have shared their ideas at conferences, in training sessions, and in their books, as well as to the tutors and students, who have added to my knowledge and given me joy and encouragement.

RJC

I SPEAK ENGLISH

A GUIDE TO TEACHING ENGLISH
TO SPEAKERS OF OTHER LANGUAGES—
LISTENING, SPEAKING, READING, WRITING

INTRODUCTION

This book of basic, professionally accepted techniques and principles is written for those who wish to help people with limited skills in English and non-English-speaking people communicate in English. Detailed instructions are provided for tutoring English to speakers of other languages on a one-to-one basis or in a small group setting. It contains simplified methods that, if applied, allow volunteers with no teaching experience to tutor effectively. *I Speak English* can also be useful to paraprofessionals and professional teachers. It is intended to be a resource to which you will want to refer as you progress as a tutor or teacher.

I Speak English is intended for instructors of ESOL worldwide. Because its primary use will be with LVA's affiliates across the United States, I have related discussions about culture essentially to this country. If you are teaching or tutoring ESOL in another country or region of the world, you will need to substitute examples of culture from those areas where I have made reference to the United States.

The need for ESOL instruction is significant. As it has been since its colonial beginnings, the United States is a country inhabited by millions of people who do not speak English. They want to learn English for many reasons: for school, work, citizenship, or for more effective interaction in environments that require proficient English communication.

In response to the increasing needs of various groups, decided to include a program of English for Speakers of Other Languages (ESOL) in 1974 to complement its Basic Literacy (BL) program, which began in 1962. Periodically, LVA updates its training materials to keep up with innovative scholarship and practice. This revision of *I Speak English* was stimulated by the research on the communicative competence theory, which focuses language learning on real-life experiences. Although it can be used independently or with other ESOL training materials, it is specifically designed to accompany LVA's tutor training workshop and will provide you with

- a theoretical and attitudinal base from which to tutor

- descriptions, demonstrations, examples, and discussions of needed skills for approaches to tutoring

- opportunities to expand these skills through practice and training

Literacy Volunteers of America, Inc.

Interwoven throughout the text and the training are six underlying themes that you can put into practice as you tutor:

1. respect for students as individuals

2. a view of tutors and students who are engaged in learning and teaching

3. sensitivity to adults' needs for immediate relevance

4. a view of tutoring and learning as collaborative activities

5. integration of language components

6. respect for individual cultures and a sensitivity to cultural differences

I invite you to join me and thousands of others across the country as we work together with people who have asked for help communicating in English. As you help others, you will also learn about other countries, other customs and traditions, other peoples, other languages. You will make new friends. You will be a part of a world building bridges between individuals, between communities and between nations. As a multicultural society, the United States is strengthened by its diversity. A truly pluralistic nation like the United States requires a good deal of tolerance and respect among all of its residents in order to flourish as a society. You will be an important link in the chain of mutual understanding between cultures.

WHY ENGLISH AS A NEW LANGUAGE?

CHAPTER

1

CHAPTER I

WHY ENGLISH AS A NEW LANGUAGE?

NEED AND DEMAND FOR ENGLISH

Why English? It is certainly not the easiest language to learn nor the most logical. However, English is the major language of technology transfer, air and space travel, and international business. It is an important medium of instruction in many countries.

Often called a "link language," English is the most widely (used)-second language in the world. People from different countries and language communities choose English more than any other language as their common medium of expression. Approximately one in six speakers in the world uses English. Statistics from The Population Bureau, Inc., indicate that between 800 million and 1 billion people (out of the over 5 billion people in the world) use the English language in some context. Nearly 400 million people speak English as a first language and 450 million people use English as their second, third, or even fourth language (Morley, 1991a).

ENGLISH FOR SPEAKERS OF OTHER LANGUAGES IN THE COMMUNITY

English is an important basic tool for people from other language communities who want to live or study in the United States or Canada. To earn a living, to have access to better jobs, to be able to enroll in training programs or institutions of higher education, or to interact with people outside one's immediate community all require the ability to understand and speak English. To thrive usually requires the additional ability to read and write English.

According to the U.S. Department of Education, one-third to one-half of those enrolled in adult education programs each year are students in ESOL classes. ESOL is the fastest-growing instructional area in adult education, even at community colleges, and there are long waiting lists for entry into many of these programs. Thousands of ESOL adults are approaching organizations like LVA for individual and small group tutoring. Many of these people are working at one or more jobs and cannot attend a more typical class.

Although many newcomers to America lead rich and rewarding lives in communities where they can rely upon their native languages, most also want to learn English. They want to communicate beyond their own cultural and language groups, to make friends in and outside their neighborhoods, to help their children with schoolwork, to participate in community events, to get better jobs, or to enroll in institutions of higher education.

ENGLISH FOR SPEAKERS OF OTHER LANGUAGES IN THE WORKPLACE

Many technical books are written in English, and because much trade and industrial terminology is in English, the demand for it is worldwide. Many adults want to learn English for their own job advancement whether they reside in the United States or not.

The need for ESOL in business and industry in the United States has been growing steadily in recent years. Companies and service industries have had to recognize the serious communication problems that have surfaced as they have hired more non-English-speaking employees at all levels—technical, business, and professional. In resettlement and vocational training programs, the need for English is paramount. Many employers hold free ESOL classes on-site to give their employees needed ESOL instruction; others refer employees to local ESOL classes or tutors.

Communication within the workplace is essential. Not only must employees be able to understand and talk to each other, but employers must know that the workers understand oral as well as written instructions. Lives can be in danger when workers cannot understand directions on the job.

Recently a local furniture-making company hired many immigrants, giving them opportunities to use and be paid for the carpentry skills they had perfected in their native countries. These workers were diligent, efficient, and willing to adapt to modern tools and machinery.

When a fire broke out in accumulated sawdust, the owners gave instructions (in English) on the loudspeakers for everyone to evacuate the buildings, to leave their posts immediately. One man from Vietnam, an excellent worker, understood little English. He didn't realize the building was on fire. He paid no attention to the loud voices and confusion, continuing to do his work at his station. The owner had to send another Vietnamese worker back into the burning building to tell him in his own language to leave the building.

After that, the owners set up English classes, stressing not only emergency and survival words, but also vocabulary related to the shop activities.

This may be an extreme example, but it dramatizes the importance of effective and timely communication in the workplace.

More and more non-English speakers are being employed in technical and professional fields. Conversely, many highly skilled professionals are working in unskilled jobs because they have serious problems communicating in English.

In addition to years of hospital experience, Boris Donetskaya had a degree in nursing from a teaching hospital in Moscow. He read and wrote English well, but his listening and speaking skills were very limited. Though he had hoped to earn money to bring his family to the United States, no hospital would hire him with his very limited ability to understand or speak English. He washed dishes at a diner while going to school to learn English.

Even those who are professionally licensed and are able to read and write English at a professional level may not be able to advance because of limited oral skills.

Work-oriented ESOL training can take place through the usual one-to-one or small group instruction in the community or at work sites, often as a result of a contract between a provider agency and an employer. In the community setting, it is usually best to integrate work-related topics with the students' other major areas of interest and need. In the work setting, instruction will usually focus more on work-related vocabulary, specific work procedures, job skills, and company goals. Even in the workplace, it is best to individualize instruction to the specific needs and interests of students and to broaden the content, while still focusing on workplace needs and issues—from both the employees' and employers' perspectives.

ENGLISH FOR SPEAKERS OF OTHER LANGUAGES IN FAMILY SETTINGS

The children of non-native English-speaking parents usually learn English more quickly and easily than their parents. In a reversal of traditional roles, children often interpret and solve problems for the parents, which sometimes creates stress in the family. This tension is common to the immigrant experience. Learning a new language does not mean abandoning the first language in the home nor a family's cultural heritage. Some parents will not need, be able, or desire to learn English. Yet for many families, when parents learn English, a mutual understanding between the generations is strengthened. The family will adjust more easily to a new culture while preserving the authenticity of its heritage as it stresses the importance of drawing on family strengths and life experiences (Auerbach, 1995). Although in many families tensions will remain, learning English can be a tool for uniting rather than dividing generations.

If one of the goals of family and intergenerational programs is to improve the scholastic achievement of children, then providing parental instruction in ESOL is a high priority. Without English, for example, parents are less able to communicate with those in the American school system. Similarly, school personnel find it difficult to understand the concerns of parents who have trouble expressing themselves in English. Parents need English to able to

- read their children's report cards and general correspondence from their schools
- meet with their children's teachers
- help their children with homework

These needs are difficult to meet without some knowledge of English.

SUMMARY

The need for teaching English to speakers of other languages is rising as the world community becomes smaller. Communication remains a key goal as people strive to coexist peacefully in communities, in the workplace, and in family settings. A common language can serve as an important tool in the development of effective communication among diverse groups of people within the United States.

◆◆◆

LANGUAGE AS COMMUNICATION

CHAPTER

11

- ♦ **NONVERBAL COMMUNICATION**

- ♦ **VERBAL COMMUNICATION** **LISTENING/ UNDERSTANDING AND SPEAKING**

- ♦ **READING AND WRITING**

- ♦ **RELATIONSHIPS AMONG THE LANGUAGE SKILLS**

- ♦ **TRENDS IN TEACHING ENGLISH TO SPEAKERS OF OTHER LANGUAGES**

- ♦ **SUMMARY**

CHAPTER II
LANGUAGE AS COMMUNICATION

Communication—the exchange of information and thoughts through verbal and nonverbal channels—is accomplished in various ways. Just how much of our time is spent communicating? According to an estimate by the New York State Department of Education, 70 percent of a person's waking time is spent communicating. The average person spends 45 percent of this communication time listening, 30 percent speaking, 16 percent reading, and 9 percent writing. Of course, these percentages vary depending on the person, but unless we are eating or sleeping, we are probably communicating.

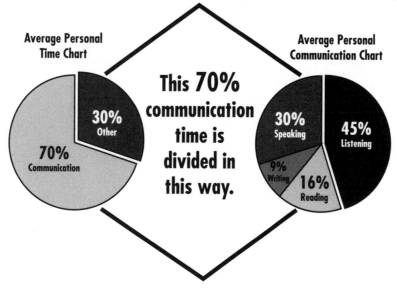

Average Personal Time Chart — 70% Communication, 30% Other. This 70% communication time is divided in this way. Average Personal Communication Chart — 45% Listening, 30% Speaking, 16% Reading, 9% Writing.

NONVERBAL COMMUNICATION

People who don't speak or understand the same language are still able to communicate.

> *We were in Swaziland recently. I wanted to visit the rural areas to observe their literacy program and see how I could help. The leaders were hesitant. I convinced them that I could handle any physical hardships, but they countered with my inability to understand or speak their native language, siSwati. I reminded them that there are many ways to communicate—with the eyes, with touch, with sensitivity to mutual concerns and problems. They agreed to take me to rural areas, where I sat on the floor in rondevals (mud huts with thatched roofs) with native Swazi women who wanted to learn to read and write. The women accepted me.*

9

We communicated at a deep and inner level, and through an interpreter I was able to work closely with them.

Since nonverbal messages differ across cultures, one needs to pay close attention to what messages students are actually sending through their body language and other signs by listening to and watching them. For example, eyes can convey friendliness or anger. Touch can show sensitivity—it often conveys comfort and support. An open hand or clasping another's hand can show friendships just as a rigid fist can show enmity or anger. A smile or a scowl can reveal inner feelings. Positive or negative feelings and attitudes do show, and the meanings of actions vary across cultures. So as you work with students, be sensitive to people's feelings and learn about and respect cultural differences.

We communicate nonverbally with our body movements—with our eyes or hands, through a look, or a pat on the back. Sometimes we are conscious of the nonverbal communication around us, but often we are not. For example, imagine I am in a restaurant. I want more coffee and have a hard time catching the server's eye. She finally sees me. I lift my empty coffee cup. She nods and then gestures, as though pouring cream, raising her eyebrows, suggesting a question. I shake my head. Without verbal communication we've communicated. The server brings me coffee without cream.

Gestures may have different connotations in different cultures. One can be totally unaware of such nonverbal communications as a raised eyebrow or a cocked head. You and your students, consciously and unconsciously, are sending communication signals. As a tutor, it is important to become aware of such signals by learning more about your students' cultures and by helping them understand some of the cultural patterns they may experience in the United States.

Music is another form of nonverbal communication. Recognition of a melody can bring a light to one's eyes, even though the words may be foreign.

In Russia, I was in a church where everything was different than in my church at home—the language, the setting, even the service. However, in the middle of the service, the congregation sang a hymn—in Russian, of course, but to a tune I recognized. I sang along in English, feeling we were communicating, certainly not in words, but through music.

Many students from other countries are vaguely aware of some American customs, such as the handshake as a greeting. Some common American gestures include waving when departing, beckoning with a forefinger, putting a finger to the lips to ask for silence, smiling to show approval, or frowning and shaking the head to show disapproval. These may or may not be known to newcomers. Common gestures in the United States may be misunderstood or ignored by students since they may have different meanings or no meaning at all in other cultures.

In order to test your own observance of nonverbal communication, watch a TV program without the sound. Can you tell what is being said? Or, at a social gathering, stand back and observe the gestures people make, without listening to their conversation. Watch how Americans use their hands; notice how close people stand to each other.

In his book *The Hidden Dimension* (1966), Edward Hall says, "We are often unaware that distances between people in the American society are significant." He suggests that Americans create an "intimate zone" or "personal zone" in which people talk together standing approximately 18 inches apart. If one person moves closer, invading this private area, the other tends to back away. This need for an intimate zone may be much closer or much further apart in other cultures, or may not exist at all.

VERBAL COMMUNICATION

The primary purpose of language is communication. In learning the English language, there are four specific skills involved:

- listening
- speaking
- reading
- writing

Listening/Understanding and Speaking

While still very young, people internalize the systems of their native languages (the forms and arrangements of words, sounds, and meanings and the basic patterns or structures). Virtually all people are able to perform two language skills in their native languages: listening and speaking. However, not all people can read and write in their own language. In fact, many of the over 5,000 or so languages throughout the world have no written system. In mastering a new language, listening and speaking skills are generally learned first. This makes sense if you consider the following:

- Children understand and speak their native language before they learn to read and write it.

- Almost all people speak and understand their native language, even though many cannot read or write them.

For our purposes, let us consider spoken language as the primary language system and the written as the secondary system. Spoken language is then reinforced by written language as some basic oral patterns are mastered. This sequence seems to be more gratifying and gives students more usable skills than the "translation" approach many of us experienced in our school language classes. How soon written language should be emphasized depends on the individual needs of students. When we begin teaching people a new language, we should consider emphasizing the spoken language. After all, in the course of a day, speaking and listening are required more than reading or writing.

Some people think that one cannot "know" a language if one cannot read or write it. This is not true. Many people understand and speak more than one language even though they cannot read or write a single word. The converse also is true. Even though a person can read and write a language, that person may not be able to speak or understand it.

READING AND WRITING

We also communicate by reading and writing words and symbols. Emergency or danger signs and labels communicate practical warnings. Signs giving directions help us find our way. Think of how much knowledge you have learned from reading alone—newspapers, textbooks, magazines, novels, biographies, mysteries, poems, history, literature, manuals, letters, signs—the list is endless. One way to respond is to take notes, impossible without the skill of writing.

RELATIONSHIPS AMONG THE LANGUAGE SKILLS

Listening and reading provide input; they are two channels for receiving information. Speaking and writing provide output; they are two channels for expressing information.

Reading and writing are communicated through written symbols, listening and speaking through aural/oral symbols. If we separate reading and writing from listening and speaking, we fragment language. All four skills are needed in the learning of English.

INPUT		OUTPUT
Listening	**SPOKEN LANGUAGE**	Speaking
Reading	**WRITTEN LANGUAGE**	Writing

TRENDS IN TEACHING ENGLISH TO SPEAKERS OF OTHER LANGUAGES

Throughout the past century and into our present time, we have learned a great deal about second (or third) language acquisition and effective teaching methods. There are several methods or approaches to teaching a new language. (A method is a specific set of procedures compatible with a given trend or approach which, in turn, is supported by certain theoretical assumptions.) *I Speak English* focuses mostly on approaches and methods used and thus includes practical exercises and activities. Some attention is given to theory to help link practice to core principles.

THE GRAMMAR TRANSLATION APPROACH, widely used until shortly after World War II, focuses on learning grammatical rules, vocabulary, and the literature of the new language. Emphasis is given to written translation rather than speaking or understanding. Little connection is made between language practice and the real-life communication needs and interests of students. Although still used, grammar translation is seldom the only method available for adult ESOL classes in the United States or Canada today.

THE AUDIOLINGUAL APPROACH, developed after World War II and popularized in the 1950s and 1960s, reflected a much-needed shift in new-language learning theory by emphasizing speaking and listening skills using repetition and oral drills with controlled materials. In audiolingual classes, greater importance is attached to pronunciation than grammatical explanation, and the first language is not used. Vocabulary is also controlled, limited to learning appropriate words in the dialogue and accompanying drills that characterize the usual audiolingual lesson.

THE COMMUNICATIVE APPROACH, also known as Communicative Language Teaching (CLT), emerged in the late 1960s and early 1970s, when the need for more practical communication among the members of the European community became apparent. It has been refined and is now used extensively in the United States. It emphasizes practical language use and stresses the importance of comprehension and the integration of all four language skills—listening, speaking, reading, and writing—through natural, authentic, real-life activities and experiences. The students take an active role in the learning situation so that the acquisition of English will be a part of their daily lives.

I Speak English advocates the Communicative Approach. Focusing on real-life situations, it uses authentic materials and emphasizes the teaching of listening with understanding and speaking, balanced with reading and writing. It also incorporates other methods. Techniques, exercises, and activities are presented to help tutors plan learner-centered, context-based lessons geared for students at varying levels from a variety of countries and cultures.

SUMMARY

Communication is a vital goal in learning a new language. It includes verbal, nonverbal, oral, and written communication. The Communicative Approach is emphasized in *I Speak English* because it focuses on real-life situations, providing students with the practical help they need.

IMPORTANCE OF CULTURE

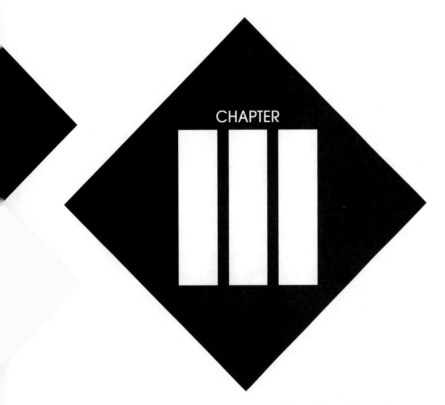

CHAPTER

III

- ◆ **DEFINITION OF CULTURE**

- ◆ **CULTURE SHOCK**

- ◆ **CULTURAL PRECONCEPTIONS**

- ◆ **SHARING OUR CULTURE**

- ◆ **LEARNING ABOUT STUDENTS' CULTURES**

- ◆ **SOME CULTURAL DIFFERENCES**

- ◆ **RESPECT FOR OTHER CULTURES**

- ◆ **SUMMARY**

CHAPTER III

IMPORTANCE OF CULTURE

Communication includes both language and culture. Words have meaning only in the context of the culture in which they are used. For example, *lift* refers to elevator in England, but in America it means to pick up. Both are English words, but because of the different cultural contexts the words have different meanings. Some languages have many ways of expressing different types of snow or rice because they are essential aspects of their cultures. Even within various areas of the United States, different words are used for the same meaning—*pail, bucket; skillet, frying pan; baby carriage, buggy.*

Learning about a new culture does not mean giving up one's native culture. But as one learns a new language in a community where other people speak that language, one learns about the community's culture as well. For years the United States was considered a "melting pot" where people from different places blended their cultures into a common American identity. More recently another view has emerged of the United States as a "mosaic" of cultures where each group of people maintains its distinctive identity while contributing to a richer, more inclusive society and culture. In the United States, the English language is a major cultural bond shared by most of the population, regardless of ethnic background.

DEFINITION OF CULTURE

Culture is a system of behaviors and beliefs. These belief systems make some things permissible under certain circumstances but nearly prohibited in others. These cultural patterns may vary from country to country and even from area to area. What may be normal or acceptable in one part of the world may be frowned upon in another. In many societies there is a generally accepted dominant culture to which many people subscribe in various ways. Yet there are often various subcultures that reflect behavioral patterns and attitudes that may be significantly different than that of the dominant culture. Culture reaches all aspects of language and communication.

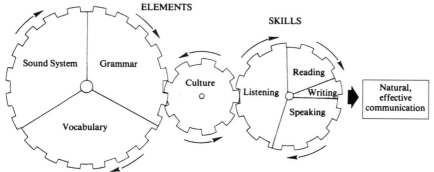

Chart from *Teaching English as a Second Language: A Self-Instructional Course.* Unit I - The Nature and Purpose of Language. Albany, N.Y. State Education Department. 1974.

CULTURE SHOCK

Culture shock is the feeling of disorientation or confusion that occurs when a person leaves a familiar place and moves to a vastly unfamiliar one.

Be aware that ESOL students might be experiencing some degree of culture shock. Outward manifestations may vary. Some people show fatigue and frustration, even hostility; others fear going out alone, depending excessively on fellow nationals for help and companionship. While some adults may feel depressed, others are stimulated. Culture shock affects different people in various ways.

CULTURAL PRECONCEPTIONS

We are products of our culture, and many of our ideas result from cultural bias. Cultural bias often causes stereotyping. For example, we may stereotype the behavior or dress of everyone in a certain group. Stereotypes are too general and too simple. Very few people fall into the "typical" picture. Members of other cultures are as individual as are members of our own culture.

For example, we may imagine all Africans living in tribal villages. However, the fact is that many Africans live in towns and cities very similar to those in the United States and have never lived in a tribal village or heard a tribal drum. Similarly, people from other countries may have preconceived ideas about life in the United States. When they think of the culture of the United States, they may envision gangsters on every street corner and cowboys riding the range and roaming across the American plains.

SHARING OUR CULTURE

People new to the United States often want to know more about the customs, attitudes, and cultural patterns of this country. As tutors, we have a responsibility to help our students learn and understand such information, which should be included in language lesson plans. Like other national groups, Americans vary from individual to individual. However, some attitudes and practices are common among most Americans.

Many Americans like being independent. They see independence as an essential aspect of freedom. Most live and treat each other quite informally with an openness that is sometimes refreshing but occasionally brusque. Americans generally value punctuality—the confusing variations on timing (appointments, plane and bus schedules, etc.) will be discussed later. In America, many women now work outside the home and have much more freedom than in previous times. We tutors may be proud of the United States and its customs, but we must not imply that American customs are the best.

LEARNING ABOUT STUDENTS' CULTURES

Many of us know little about the customs, cultures, and even the locations of other countries. As you learn new perspectives and gain more information from your students, you will probably want to learn more about their native lands from them.

Learning a new language and trying to adapt to a new culture are difficult tasks, and the process can be frustrating. It is important that ESOL tutors empathize with students. Becoming acquainted with your students' native countries and cultures can help build the needed rapport between you and your students. Such interest on your part is important to build long-term relationships and indicates a sincere interest in your students as individuals. A little knowledge can prevent your unknowingly offending your students.

It is useful to read books and articles about your students' countries, cultures, and languages to help you to understand and appreciate the differences between your and your students' cultures. In addition to maps, novels, and articles in *National Geographic,* which contain invaluable information on nearly every country, check with your local librarian for other resources on specific peoples and countries.

An informative and useful tool to help tutors understand specific culture and language differences is *CULTURGRAMS,* a collection of information about individual countries published by Brigham Young University, Provo, Utah. If you have access to a computer and the Internet, you can search the World Wide Web to get background information on many countries. There are many sources (books, articles, television, videos, CD ROMS, and the Internet) that provide substantial knowledge of different cultures. Be sure to draw on this important material. An understanding of culture is not optional. It should help you understand your students and be a part of your teaching.

SOME CULTURAL DIFFERENCES

It would be impossible to detail all the cultural differences around the world, but you should be sensitive to the fact that differences exist. Greetings, for example, vary from culture to culture. The American *Hi! How are ya?* or a wave of the hand indicate an informal friendliness. In some cultures, it is polite to be more formal and to inquire about the health of each member of the family. Handshaking is common in many cultures, but it is done in different ways— sometimes firm and brisk, other times limp and relaxed. Another approach is to grab the thumb and wrist with a hearty verbal greeting. In some cultures, a kiss on both cheeks is the familiar greeting by both men and women. In some Asian cultures, the custom is to place the palms of one's hands together and give a slight bow. Americans and Asians generally limit touching to a handshake. Latinos tend toward a "touching culture," greeting each other with hugs, kisses, vigorous handshakes, and pats on the back.

When being introduced in America, a woman may offer her hand or may simply nod. She might say, *How do you do?* or just *Hi!* Men more generally greet with a handshake. Teenagers greet each other more casually. Your students will need to know how to recognize the occasion for each behavior. Much will depend on relative social status, age, gender, or perhaps on the circumstances of the moment. If your students are newcomers, you may want to try practicing greetings in role-playing situations.

Facial expressions convey various meanings in different cultures. Surprise or shock among people in the United States is often shown by opening the eyes wide and raising the eyebrows. To a Chinese, this is often a sign of anger, while to a Puerto Rican, it can be a sign of lack of understanding. In Asia, respect for teachers, the elderly, and people in high positions is often shown by casting eyes downward. Adult Americans of any age and status, on the other hand, expect others always to look them in the eye.

The accepted distance between people conversing is influenced by culture. People from some parts of the world, especially Latin America, feel comfortable standing close to one another. In conversation with an American, the Latino may feel snubbed and consider the American aloof because of the American's distance, while an American may feel stifled by the Latino's closeness.

According to McMichael and Coor (1983), American gestures and body movements may be offensive to people of other cultures. These include

- hands on hips, slouching
- sitting on a desk
- yawning
- stretching
- counting people with index finger and wide arm movement
- beckoning with index finger or pointing to a person with the left hand
- giving anything with the left hand

To many East Asians, these actions are not acceptable:

- touching a person of the opposite sex
- touching a person on the head
- passing something over someone's head
- wearing revealing clothes

To many Arabs, these actions are offensive:

- touching or hugging a person of the opposite sex
- sitting so that the sole of your foot is exposed
- giving something (especially food) with your left hand
- turning your back on someone during conversation
- winking

Just knowing some of the cultural codes may help you become sensitive to your students' outlooks as you work together.

In many cultures, great emphasis is put on hospitality. Sharing food is an important way of showing friendship and gratitude. In cultures where great importance is put on maintaining a close extended family, any relative, no matter how distant, has the right to ask for hospitality. In the United States, it is acceptable for dinner guests to arrive five or ten minutes later than the time set, but not an hour late or early. However, job candidates should arrive a little early (e.g., five minutes) for an interview. American time standards vary, depending on the situation.

Teachers are held in high regard in many countries. Sometimes this attitude is so prevalent that students feel the teacher is always right and knows all the answers. Students need to know that this would be impossible for anyone. If you do not know answers to some of their questions, admit it, and tell your students that you will attempt to find the answers. Also, students should know that we are all engaged in learning and teaching, and that we have much to learn from each other.

Even advanced ESOL students may not understand the cultural differences between their homelands and the United States that they will encounter. Your students will appreciate your sensitive help.

RESPECT FOR OTHER CULTURES

It is important never to take lightly another culture's way of doing things. As much as possible, keep an open mind and avoid value judgments when dealing with cultural differences. Instead, show honest interest, learning all you can about your students' backgrounds. It can be fun to taste native dishes of other countries and to learn about their customs and holidays. One culture is not better than another—just different.

SUMMARY

If you are conscious of the importance of cultural understanding and if you obtain a basic grasp of effective techniques and approaches for teaching ESOL, you are on your way to becoming an effective tutor. You will likely become a more sensitive person in your day-to-day life, thereby enriching all of your life experiences.

Getting to know at least one person from another country with a different language helps expand one's awareness of the great variety of human experiences. Just as the one person you meet represents his or her country and its customs, you may be the only person from your culture with whom your students get well acquainted. Accordingly, you represent a "typical" person from your country or culture to your students—quite a challenge for each of us!

◆◆◆

LEARNERS AND TUTORS

CHAPTER

IV

- ◆ **WHO ARE THOSE WHO WANT TO LEARN ENGLISH?**
  IMMIGRATION PATTERNS

  REASONS FOR LEARNING ENGLISH

  PROFILE OF ESOL STUDENTS

- ◆ **WHO ARE THOSE WHO WANT TO TEACH?**
  WHY PEOPLE WANT TO TEACH

  IS THERE A NEED TO KNOW THE STUDENTS' LANGUAGES?

  PROFILE OF EFFECTIVE ESOL TUTORS

- ◆ **SUMMARY**

CHAPTER IV
LEARNERS AND TUTORS

WHO ARE THOSE WHO WANT TO LEARN ENGLISH?

North America is a land of immigrants. Our ancestors came to the United States from other countries and lands. We like to think of them with nostalgia and fond memories. They brought a rich heritage to their new homeland. But if they hadn't learned to communicate in English, they would have had difficulty learning new ideas or sharing much of their traditional life with people from different language groups or communicating outside their communities in the United States. English was and still is the common language for general communication among the diverse groups that make up American society.

Newly arrived foreigners may be viewed with suspicion and mistrust, with pity and compassion, or perhaps with friendliness and generosity. Their lives have been transplanted from a familiar native land to the United States, where they may face a new language, a different lifestyle, strange foods, unfamiliar government, homesickness for friends and family, and often an immediate need for employment. All these combine to make life very difficult indeed.

Immigration Patterns

Native American Indians migrated to North America thousands of years ago. Some groups, such as Africans, were transported and enslaved. Most others came by choice. For a variety of economic, political, or religious reasons, these immigrants saw the New World as a place for a better life.

The Spanish, Portuguese, English, and French were followed by the Dutch, German, Irish, Swedish, and Scottish people. Since most of the colonies followed the English customs of law and government, and the people in power spoke English, English became the dominant language used in America.

Between 1890 and 1924, approximately twenty million people arrived in America, mostly from China and eastern and southern Europe: Slovaks, Hungarians, Serbs, Poles, Ukrainians, Russians, Greeks, and Italians. Subsequent waves of immigrants just preceding and following World War II brought more people from Eastern Europe, South America, Mexico, India, Pakistan, the Caribbean islands, and East Asia. More recently, millions of refugees have immigrated to the United States—Cubans, Vietnamese, Cambodians, Haitians, Salvadorans, Nicaraguans, Laotians, Russians, Bosnians, and Somalis.

Often communities developed when immigrants with similar backgrounds lived in the same area. These communities currently exist in all major American and Canadian cities. Historically, Scandinavians and Germans settled in Minnesota and the Dakotas. Many immigrants stayed near their ports of entry: Cubans in Florida, Asians in California (as well as along the railroad lines across Canada), French in Quebec, Mexicans in southern California and Texas. Often, after a family first settled in the United States, they decided to move to a different state to be closer to a larger, similar ethnic community or to find a climate closer to that of their native country. Immigrants often brought with them a particular skill or trade and traveled to settle in the place where their talents could be utilized and where relatives and friends were already established in similar jobs. It seems to be human nature to want to go where you have friends and relatives, where someone understands your customs and knows your language, or where you can find familiar work.

People from around the world continue to come to the United States and Canada either to live, visit, or study for a period of time. If they don't know how to speak and understand English, it is difficult for them to get jobs, to make medical appointments, or even to shop.

Reasons for Learning English

We previously described general needs and demands for English in the community, workplace, and family. Individual students have specific motivations for learning English. For example:

1. They need life skills to be able to survive and function in their new country—to be able to go shopping, find adequate housing, communicate with medical personnel, answer the telephone, understand the media, and deal with the banking and credit system of their new country.

    Prany and Souk were refugees from Laos, living in a midwestern city. They had two small children and lived in a tiny apartment with only essential furniture and clothing. Prany tried to remember how to get to the local market, but she got lost. Because he knew no English, she couldn't ask directions and found her way home only by chance. When she went shopping, she picked out only familiar foods and held out her American money, hoping the cashier wouldn't cheat her.

2. They want to get jobs. For example, a factory worker needs to be able to follow instructions in English. An accountant from one country may find himself working as a maintenance worker in the United States because he cannot transfer his work skills to the English-speaking job market.

    Juan Vargas came to the United States from Mexico to get a better job and find more opportunities for his family. He could not understand or speak English. He worried about venturing out on a bus when he could not ask directions or understand anyone. He also thought he could not even apply for a menial job if he could not communicate in English.

3. They need additional academic training. People who are well educated and can read and write English fluently often need help with oral communication skills. Others who have received degrees or certification in their home countries sometimes find that their credentials are not sufficient for employment in the United States.

   Shen taught civil engineering at a university in China. He passed the written English tests and was enrolled at an American university to do graduate work. Although Shen could read the required books in English, he could not follow the lectures and was getting further and further behind in class. He could not ask his fellow students for assistance because he could not understand English.

4. They want to make friends in this new country.

   Hidaat was a Fulbright scholar from Eritrea, a small country in northern Africa. She was the only person from her country at her American university. She was the only person who spoke Eritrean, and since she spoke and understood little English, there was no one there with whom she could talk. Because of her halting English and shy nature, she found it difficult to talk with strangers, even students in her classes.

5. They want to become citizens and need help to pass the citizenship test.

   Chiang Ping came to the United States from Hong Kong several years ago. He has been working diligently on English. Mr. Chiang's job as a checkout clerk in a local supermarket has given him opportunities to practice his listening and speaking skills. He is now studying the history of the United States and learning about the workings of its government as he prepares to take the examination to become an American citizen.

6. They want to be able to speak English with other members of their family.

   Marta came to America to be with her son and his wife and their American-born children. Marta spoke only Spanish. Even though her son and his wife spoke Spanish, their children most often spoke English, and Marta felt left out of most of the family activities.

7. They want to help their children in school.

   Tatiana was a high school teacher from Russia. As she watched her son struggle with his homework, she knew she could help him more if only she knew English. She knew how important it was for parents to communicate with and work closely with their children's teachers. How could she attend a teacher-parent conference without knowing English?

8. They realize how important knowing English can be to their personal safety.

   Rescue workers at a car accident were frustrated because it was difficult to communicate with injured migrant workers to ask where they hurt, to tell them not to move, and to assure them that an ambulance would take them to the hospital. Interpreters were recruited at the hospital, but at the scene of the accident, the injured were frightened because they couldn't understand their rescuers' instructions. They realized that understanding and speaking English in America could be of critical importance.

Profile of ESOL Students

There is, of course, no "typical" ESOL student. As a tutor, you should become as informed as possible about your students. They may be male or female, young or old, with no formal education or with advanced degrees. They may come from various ethnic, religious, and economic backgrounds, some knowing much about the United States and its history, others knowing almost nothing. Sometimes they have misinformation and false ideas about Americans, which eventually need to be amended.

Common Characteristics among ESOL Learners

Most adult ESOL learners

- need friendship and acceptance
- fear embarrassment
- experience stress in their new surroundings
- have responsibilities in addition to learning English
- are highly motivated
- have differing backgrounds
- have difficulty pronouncing certain sounds
- have problems understanding English-speakers

Need Friendship and Acceptance

Most of us are so involved in our own daily lives that we forget that there are people living in the community who really need to be accepted as neighbors and friends, not just allowed to live nearby. This is illustrated in the following incident:

Two travelers stopped at a small diner for a sandwich. The woman and the two men working there had heavy foreign accents. Conversation between us brought out the fact that they were Greek, had been in the United States for six years, had some family back in Greece, and loved living in America. They had become citizens and were proud of it, but they couldn't understand many aspects of American life. They wanted and needed someone to explain and discuss with them American holiday customs, politics, schools, and parent organizations. Almost of all their associations were with other family members, and it was difficult for them to become part of a larger American community. They felt they couldn't take the initiative to meet new people. Invitations to American homes would have been most welcome.

As Americans, we can and should become sensitive to the need newcomers have for friendship and acceptance. In doing so we enrich ourselves and our own lives.

Fear Embarrassment

Students often hesitate to try speaking English because they fear making mistakes. You can instill confidence in them by making your lessons progress at a pace compatible with their abilities. Small successes in beginning lessons can build to bigger successes as students realize they are communicating in English.

Experience Stress in Their New Surroundings

Many non-English-speaking persons are scared to try to speak any English. Knowing only a few words, such as *hello* and *thank you,* is not enough to last through a community meeting or a session at the employment agency. When one needs help in an emergency, it can be a frightening experience not to be able to explain what is wrong. On the other hand, some non-English-speaking persons may seem loud and boisterous. Often this is a defense mechanism to cover up a lack of confidence. People react to stress in many different ways.

Have Responsibilities in Addition to Learning English

Newcomers to America have responsibilities beyond learning English. They are concerned about where to live, how to find a job, and how to care for their families. Tutors must take these responsibilities seriously. You can do so by integrating concerns your students have about their lives into your lessons as long as you and the students are comfortable doing so.

Are Highly Motivated

Most ESOL students are highly motivated. They realize why they need to learn English. Many know what they want to learn and are persistent about learning it. Their motivation enhances their ability to learn English.

Success in learning a new language depends not only on innate ability, but also to a great extent on whether an individual wants to learn and feels capable of learning. How quickly a person may learn to understand and speak English will depend on many things, such as the person's ability to absorb a new language, the amount of time she spends with people who speak English, and the individual's personality and level of persistence. Some students may feel they are not learning fast enough, which might make them more driven or in need of extra encouragement.

Have Differing Backgrounds

Like all others, ESOL students are shaped by their backgrounds. One student may have had extensive education and come from a family of high stature. She may resent her new situation. She may even seem arrogant. Another student may come from very modest means. He may be here without his family. Often an entire family has pooled its resources to send just one member of their family to the United States to work toward a better life. Whatever your students' backgrounds, it is up to you as a tutor to help them set and achieve their own goals of learning English and understanding more about their new culture.

Have Difficulty Pronouncing Certain Sounds

Adults with excellent formal education often have difficulty speaking the English language intelligibly. Producing certain sounds and stress patterns characteristic of spoken English may present a major difficulty for some because these sounds do not even exist in their native language.

Each language has its own sound system. Some African languages have click sounds. French has some vowel sounds that are difficult for learners. Native English-speakers have as much trouble imitating these sounds as speakers of other languages do some English sounds. Learning to speak another language often requires a whole new set of muscular movements to make the appropriate sounds and involves a new set of stress and intonation patterns.

Have Problems Understanding English Speakers

Many ESOL students can read and write English, can even repeat English words well, but cannot understand what is said to them. Asking questions that require more than a yes or no answer can help tutors know if students comprehend. Native English speakers use many contractions, slur words together (*Wha-cha-do-in,* means *What are you doing?*), and use colloquial phrases, idioms, and slang. These language patterns are incomprehensible to ESOL students at first and can be very frustrating. Much empathy is needed.

Summary of Learners' Characteristics

Whoever your students are, whatever their backgrounds, whatever abilities or weaknesses they show, you must be sensitive to each individual's real needs and interests. By using the "how to" skills which are taught later in this book, along with your own insights, you can help someone communicate in English and live a fuller life. Let your students know that learning English may open many doors for them.

If a student speaks no English and can understand nothing you say at first, be patient. If you start simply and build slowly, little successes will bring a flash of comprehension when understanding does come. If you are the first person with whom your students can communicate in English, you will have become a very important person in their lives—a real reward for you both!

WHO ARE THOSE WHO WANT TO TEACH?

Why People Want to Teach

Some people want to travel, to learn about other cultures, and to meet people from other countries, but have not had the opportunity. Meeting and working with people from other countries by teaching them English can open up the world without travel. Others have plans of going to other countries through the Peace Corps or a church mission group. They know that English teaching skills will be useful, and they want to learn those skills now—not only to get valuable experience that fits in with their plans, but to have the chance to help someone else immediately.

Some people seem to be born teachers. Some were professional teachers and either want to continue in retirement or want to supplement their teaching of children by teaching adults. Some have had no teaching experience but know they would like to try. Still others have heard the stories of their grandparents who came to America from another country, lonely, frightened, knowing no English. They feel they are giving back something that was probably given to their ancestors. Tutoring ESOL students provides an opportunity for anyone to teach.

Whatever your motives, the desire to help and the willingness to give time to tutoring, while very important, are not enough. Learning the strategies and techniques for teaching English to speakers of other languages; learning how to assess students' strengths, needs, interests, and goals; and learning how to plan lessons are all essential to effective tutoring. This book and LVA's accompanying tutor training workshop provide many practical tools.

Is There a Need to Know the Students' Languages?

One question continually arises with regard to tutoring students who speak little or no English: How important is it for the tutor to speak and understand students' native languages? Most tutors will not know their students' languages. It is not necessary for the tutor to have this knowledge. Knowing some words in a student's native language can be useful for explaining a difficult concept or giving directions, but it can also be a crutch to lean on. When students and the tutor speak the same language, they may revert too often to that language instead of stretching to use English.

Certainly you should not avoid your student's language completely. There are obvious advantages to knowing your student's language—the ease in explaining an abstract term and the security of sharing a common language. The use of a bilingual dictionary (English and your student's native language) can be helpful, providing your student can read his or her native language. It might be too time-consuming to spend ten minutes attempting to act out the meaning of a difficult word like *develop* or *justice* when you could explain it in the native language or look it up in a bilingual dictionary. Learning some words in your student's language can also help build rapport, especially when your pronunciation is not quite correct.

Another question often arises: Should tutors try to learn students' languages as they teach? Except for learning a few phrases and showing that you, too, experience difficulty in trying to learn another language, We suggest not, at least not from your student. Your student came to the program to learn English, not to participate in language exchange.

Profile of Effective ESOL Tutors

Throughout history, individuals have made a difference—sometimes for good and sometimes for evil. Don't underestimate the extent of your own influence, even on one person. Don't worry if you are not a professional teacher. The quality of the teacher-learner relationship often makes the difference between an effective and a frustrating teaching/learning experience. The basic ingredients of this relationship are good communication skills, (particularly active listening), the ability to help your students learn to speak effectively, and, above all, empathy.

Whatever your previous training, some of the skills you already have will help you to learn the new teaching skills you need. Technical skills that encompass practical methods for teaching English are crucial—but equally important are patience, enthusiasm, creativity, adaptability, and respect for your student.

Characteristics of ESOL Tutors

Effective tutors

- are well trained
- are learner-centered
- plan and keep records
- exhibit the following personal qualities
  - ◆ understanding and respect
  - ◆ patience
  - ◆ adaptability
  - ◆ enthusiasm and encouragement
  - ◆ sense of humor
  - ◆ cultural sensitivity
  - ◆ creativity

♦ accountability
♦ responsibility
♦ realistic expectations
♦ commitment

Training

How can you prepare yourself to tutor someone to speak, understand, read, and write English? Just an ability to understand, speak, read, and write English won't suffice. Learning the skills and techniques for teaching ESOL and making well-thought-out lesson plans are essential to becoming an effective tutor.

LVA offers training in tutoring to get the skills needed to teach English. The training is a professionally designed and field-tested workshop. The workshop has been developed especially for nonprofessionals whose fields are other than ESOL, but can be used by professionals in the field as well. *I Speak English* is the handbook that accompanies the workshop. Together, they provide the skills and practice needed to become an effective tutor.

Other workshops and college courses preparing tutors and teachers to work with ESOL students are offered in many communities. There may be conferences of ESOL teachers offered by local chapters of TESOL (Teachers of English to Speakers of Other Languages) that you can attend. Your local literacy program may also offer in-service workshops. All such training opportunities increase one's skills in helping someone learn to understand, speak, read, and write English. You will get new insights and learn new techniques by continuing to seek out training opportunities.

Learner-Centeredness

Learner-centered tutoring is directly related to the students' needs and goals. It means keeping students' needs at the heart of instruction and seeing students as partners in the learning process. Effective tutors must be attuned to their students' goals and immediate needs so that lessons can be designed to address these needs and goals. Students need to gain their own skills, not to see a demonstration of the skills the tutor possesses. Tutors must show how, not show off. Specific techniques for teaching learner-centered, communicative skills will be discussed in detail later.

Planning and Keeping Records

As a volunteer tutor, you are responsible for planning your students' lessons with input from your students, for teaching, and for keeping records. Your main job is to help your students expand their new skills, and each session must be an opportunity to help your students learn more English. Because there never seems to be enough time for all you anticipate doing, plan your lessons carefully. Make the most of your time together. Keep a good mixture of review, new learning, and fun. Stay on task. Do not try to solve all of your students' personal problems. Often after concentrating on the lesson and meeting some success in learning English, students can view personal problems with new hope and understanding.

Personal Qualities

Understanding and Respect

Your students may have had problems finding a place to live, getting a job, and even functioning in everyday ways. They may have found it hard to use local transportation, to buy food, or to get help in an emergency. Successful tutors understand that students overcome many obstacles every day, and they respect their efforts and abilities.

Patience

Effective tutors have many virtues, but perhaps the greatest of these is patience. Sometimes learning may seem very slow, but there are times when all the carefully built knowledge seems to come together at once, and the student suddenly says, *Oh, I see.* Stepping stones allow them to eventually function independently, using English in new situations. The patient work becomes worthwhile, and the joy of learning is realized by both the tutor and the student.

Adaptability

People are infinitely different. Some have phenomenal memories; others have keen intuition; some have a knack of learning through observation; and some are patient plodders who will learn if you are patient enough to allow them time. Your challenge is to adapt your teaching to your students' learning styles. Be open-minded to new ideas and plan a variety of teaching techniques.

Enthusiasm and Encouragement

Keep your enthusiasm high and give genuine encouragement to your students. Most often a feeling of achievement with small successes must occur before long-term success can be established. However, do not pretend success when both of you know that it has not been achieved. Excessive excitement and urging are not conducive to real learning, but genuine respect for each student's growth can be a source of help and pride.

Tutors often blame themselves if their students are not learning English quickly enough, but there are many reasons why the pace may be slower than you or your students would like. Try not to take this personally, but remind yourself that each student's "one step at a time" often consists of tiny steps. To empathize, advise, and teach without becoming disillusioned presents a delicate balancing act for tutors.

Encourage students to use English not only in their lessons but also in their daily lives. Suggest that listening to TV and radio programs can be good practice in hearing and understanding the spoken language as well as an effective way to gather information. Remind your students that participation in other small group conversations is helpful and that other classes might be available in their communities for further study and reinforcement.

Sense of Humor

A tough task is often made easier by including some light moments. Laughter often reduces tension, and sharing a good joke is a fine way to build a relationship and to add pleasure to some otherwise hard work. A teaching hour with several laughs in it will seem like a much shorter time. When you laugh, be sure your students are laughing with you. Remember, adults can be very sensitive, especially in areas where they feel insecure and inadequate. Try learning—pronouncing and remembering—a few words in your student's language. That should provide a laugh as well as keep you reminded of the difficulties in being the student.

Cultural Sensitivity

ESOL tutors need to be sensitive to what students are facing. If you have traveled or lived in another country without knowing the language of that country, you know how difficult even everyday activities can be. Some tutors may be immigrants themselves and thus understand some of the real problems, frustrations, and dreams of newcomers. But most of us have not had this experience and must try to compensate by educating ourselves about our students' cultures and by being aware of both our verbal and nonverbal interactions with them.

Students may need explanations about some of the cultural systems of their new country. Little things you take for granted should be shared with your students. Students are more likely to feel comfortable and more easily accepted if they know the general cultural patterns of the adopted country. They are then free to choose for themselves how they will respond to them. By the same token, knowing some of the cultural patterns of your students' countries will help you find similarities to and contrasts with those of your own. You can learn about these through your reading as well as through discussions with students.

Creativity

This book encourages tutor creativity. Individualized lessons are most effective when you use the basic techniques and exercises as a springboard to your own creative endeavors. Use your own imagination as your confidence in your teaching skills increases. Don't overlook ESOL textbooks. Imaginatively used, they can be an excellent basis for instruction. Once you feel comfortable with the basics, the next step toward creativity becomes easier. Every technique and exercise can be adapted to individual needs.

Accountability

You are accountable to your sponsoring organization for giving reports on the progress of your students. Before you plan a new lesson, it is helpful to write up what has happened in the past lesson. These records will give you an ongoing report of your students' progress throughout the year, making yearly reports much easier. Your notes can be kept in individual student folders or portfolios, and you should share these with your students periodically. You are indeed accountable to each other to prepare for lessons and to communicate with each other in a timely way about schedule changes or postponements of tutoring sessions.

Responsibility

Success stories are stimulating, but not all students are equally successful at learning English. Some are highly motivated to learn the new language. Others seem less so, for many reasons. Your responsibility is to act as a sounding board for some of the common problems that ESOL students face. Respond with timely lessons that, whenever possible, draw upon issues students face. You are not expected to help students solve every problem they may face. Your primary task remains teaching English through relevant content.

Realistic Expectations

As a tutor you have a responsibility to help your students become independent as quickly as possible. Yet you must be realistic. To set goals too far above a person's current abilities and to expect endless hours of study when a student has home responsibilities and a full-time job is not practical. There are a number of reasons that people learn at different rates. Consider these factors:

- Some students need considerable repetition; others absorb and remember almost everything right away.

- The first language of some students may be much like English; the first language of other students may use a different alphabet and have few words, if any, similar to English.

- Some students have many opportunities to practice their English outside of class; others do not.

- Some students may have prior experience learning other languages.

Whatever the ease or difficulty of learning, treat your students as individuals with due allowance for differences in rate and style of learning.

You may be easily discouraged if you measure your students' progress by your own standards in learning other things. Remember, language learning is hard work. If you've ever tried to learn a foreign language, think back to your own attempts. Patience and praise for small successes probably did much to encourage you to continue trying. The same principle holds for all learners.

Commitment

An effective tutor makes a real commitment to the job. Your work will pay off in tangible and intangible ways. A teaching commitment requires

1. training—mastering techniques for teaching ESOL

2. planning—setting long-and short-range goals with your students and writing out lesson plans that will work toward meeting those goals

3. dedication—teaching one student or small group for at least two hours each week for a minimum of a year

4. accountability—keeping progress records and reporting them to your sponsoring organization

SUMMARY

You are not expected to solve every personal problem your students have, but perhaps you can steer your students to someone who can help. You certainly need to respect them as adults who are overcoming real problems as they try to improve their ability to communicate in English. A motivated learner and a creative, trained teacher who is willing to adapt and offer practical instruction make a winning combination. Learning a new language can be an exciting adventure. What is best for one student may not always be right for another. Individualize your teaching by adapting your teaching methods, activities, and materials to meet individual needs. This can be done even when tutoring several students.

While many ESOL tutors are native English-speakers, it's a real advantage to have learned English as a new language yourself, especially if you've come from the same language community as the students assigned to you. Because you've faced similar struggles, you can offer keen insights into the needs, goals, and problems your students identify, making yourself a role model for them.

LEARNING AND TEACHING

CHAPTER

V

CHAPTER V
LEARNING AND TEACHING

NATURE OF LANGUAGE

Effective acquisition of a new language is not only a mental process but an emotional and social one as well, since language is a part of culture, and learning involves the whole person in community with others. This chapter considers some of these diverse processes in the following discussion on speech patterns, learning styles, and collaborative learning—whether through small group or one-to-one instruction.

The purpose of this book is not to describe fully the components of English grammar, but rather to help new tutors understand some specific aspects of the English language that will aid them in their tutoring. Thus, the following discussion of language is geared toward the immediate needs of tutors. We will concentrate on the significance of the following:

- dialects, accents, and styles of speaking

- vocabulary and sentence structure

- stress, rhythm, and intonation patterns

Dialects, Accents, and Styles of Speaking

Oral language is a system of meaningful sounds used to communicate. These sounds are meaningful because they are produced in a patterned way that is mutually understood by speakers of the same language.

To get a clearer idea of what it means to say that oral language is a system of meaningful sounds having patterns, think of these three kinds of sounds:

a. Noises in traffic or at a construction site: These are a jumble of sounds with no particular pattern or structure.

b. People talking in a foreign tongue: These sounds are understood by some people but probably not by you. The sounds follow a regular pattern and thus have structure. You just don't know the structural pattern or the meaning of the sounds.

c. People talking in English: These sounds are organized in such a way that if you know English structure and vocabulary, you can understand the meaning. A person who does not speak or understand English cannot isolate words from among the streams of sound. For communication to take place, both the speaker and the listener must know the subsystems—vocabulary, structure, sounds, stress, rhythm, and intonation patterns—inherent in that language. Each subsystem has its own set of rules. Some of the rules which govern the English systems are different from rules which govern other language systems.

English, like other languages, has dialects or varieties. Are American and British English different dialects of the same language? What about accents—a Brooklyn accent, a southern accent, a midwestern accent?

Most of us use formal and informal styles of speaking, depending upon the situation. Words that are proper in one situation or setting may not be accepted in another. Speech used in introducing a guest speaker is usually more formal, while speech used during a family outing is more informal. Informal styles often include language with multiple meanings, with idioms, even slang. Technical language could be an example of one type of formal language. Every professional group has its own specialty words or jargon. Thus, practical English must be adaptable. It is the responsibility of the tutor to explain the different ways English is used and to work with students to identify the various frameworks in which they need to understand and speak English.

Vocabulary and Sentence Structure

The vocabulary of a language is a collection of the words of that language. These words can refer to particular objects, actions, or feelings, or they can be modifiers or connecting words. Vocabulary expansion is an important part of learning a language. As tutors, we must be aware that the vocabulary needs of individual students must be addressed. For example, the vocabulary required by an engineer may be very different from the vocabulary needed by a farmer, a nurse, or a new mother, even though they are all using the same language.

The structure of a language is the relationship between words and parts of words, including the order of the words used to convey the intended meaning. Syntax is another word for sentence structure. For example, *The dog chased the boy* has meaning for speakers of English partially because of the order of the words. We know who is doing the chasing because the noun *dog* comes before the verb *chased*. Compare that with *The boy chased the dog*. As another example, consider the difference in *He trains seals* and *He seals trains*. Many of us cannot remember the names of the parts of speech, and we may not be able to state the rules that apply to correct usage. However, we understand what is said because we know the vocabulary and recognize the pattern or structure. Because structure is so important in English, you will need to help your students learn it.

Stress, Rhythm, and Intonation Patterns

In addition to the sounds in words, the way words are pronounced also conveys meaning, as does the way words are stressed in sentences. Depending on which word is stressed, a sentence can take on a different meaning. For example, *JOE drove the car home* (not Bill or Bob). *Joe DROVE the car home* (he didn't push it or have it towed). *Joe drove the CAR home* (not the jeep or the bike). *Joe drove the car HOME* (not to the garage or to school).

Each language has a rhythm of its own. Some are more pulsating, like music, while others are more staccato. Living in an area where the language you are learning is spoken gives opportunities to feel the language's rhythm subconsciously.

Intonation is sometimes called the melody of a language. It refers to the pitch changes used in speaking. These intonation patterns play an important role in conveying meaning. For example, *Joe DROVE the car home?* (After the accident, it wasn't in such bad shape that he couldn't? Unbelievable!) Other languages have pitch assigned to each word. In Chinese, for example, the word *ma* can mean *mom, numbness,* or *horse,* depending on the tone.

LEARNING AND TEACHING STYLES

Some people are visual learners. Others learn best through listening. Some learn best when they combine actions with speaking. And others learn best through reading and writing. It's important to be sensitive to your students' learning styles and be aware of your own style of teaching/learning.

You may want to look at your own approach to learning. Do you prefer to look at a problem or a lesson as a whole, and then examine the parts? Or do you prefer to look at the smaller pieces or parts of a problem or lesson before exposing yourself to the bigger picture? Your students will vary in their learning preferences because people do not all learn in the same way.

Alice Omaggio Hadley (1993) suggests that students as well as tutors have differing needs, styles, and preferences. Some people learn best through the senses—the ears, the eyes, touch, movement. Some people prefer learning with others, interacting in small groups, while others seem to learn best doing individual projects. Some learners thrive on exciting and creative new settings while others prefer structured guidance. Tutors should be sensitive to all of these differences.

Some students are extremely shy, tending not to talk when in a group, especially with members of the opposite sex. Others want to talk continuously, dominating the group. As much as possible, it is up to the tutor to encourage equal participation by directing questions to shy students and gently letting the more vocal students know that all students must be given opportunities to speak.

How a teacher approaches learning situations affects how students learn. Teachers may use a responsive, collaborative, learner-directed way of teaching or a more controlling, teacher-directed way. Both learner-directed and teacher-directed approaches can be effective, and teachers often practice an eclectic approach, incorporating elements of both.

Some students will expect an exclusively teacher-directed approach, since this is probably the way they were taught as children. However, experience has shown that the learner-centered approach is usually more effective when working with adults. In the beginning, tutors may want to consider adjusting their teaching styles to conform completely to their students' learning styles. Sometimes the students' styles and the tutors' styles are already similar. Sometimes they are exactly opposite. Over time, the tutor and the students will likely adjust to each other's styles.

How can a tutor find the best ways for individual students to learn when they speak and understand only limited English or no English at all? One way is to observe which ways seem most comfortable for the students and which ways they seem to learn and retain the most. Or you can ask them. Do they seem to learn better by seeing pictures, by experiencing an event (going to a market, walking through a kitchen identifying objects), by hearing (from radio or TV), by memorizing (repeating again and again), or by writing (as a reinforcement to the speaking and hearing)? You will want to concentrate on their best learning styles, but you will also want to introduce different learning styles since students can benefit from using a diversity of approaches to learning.

It is often difficult to pair up teachers and students who have the same teaching and learning styles. To establish an effective learning climate, teachers must learn to blend their teaching styles with their students' learning styles. Yet students need to stretch a bit, too. Adrianne Bonham (1988) suggests that learners be encouraged "to expand their style range rather than seek only comfortable experiences." Learners as well as tutors benefit from style flexibility.

Whatever the teaching and learning styles of tutors and students, learning is most effective when sensitive and careful planning, a willingness to adapt, and enthusiasm and patience are a part of each session. Your goal is to build success into each lesson. Even small successes give positive reinforcement to your students. You are trying to help them become self-sufficient so they can function more effectively using English in real-life situations outside the tutoring session.

SMALL GROUPS AND ONE-TO-ONE

ESOL is taught in classes, in small groups, and one-to-one. This book focuses on small groups and one-to-one teaching, although the same methods can apply with larger groups.

Small Groups

Tutoring students in a small group—as opposed to one to one—can have many advantages. For example, less pressure is put on the individual to perform or respond to every question. Students also learn from each other. Tutors can set up more authentic activities through role-playing that approximate the use of English outside the class. I suggest that a small group consist of three to five students. If the students are from the same country, they can feel the moral support of their compatriots. They can discuss successes or problems in their native language and encourage each other, but they should interact in English in class.

Having students from different countries in the same group can also be an advantage. It would be impossible for them to speak to each other in their native languages in class. Because they must speak English, they tend to progress faster. And they learn that they are not the only ones having problems with pronunciation, comprehension, reading, or writing. The faster ones can help the slower ones. Often students are stimulated as they see learning from several viewpoints.

Tutors who have worked with small groups as opposed to one-to-one often feel it is more rewarding to work with small groups. They can help more learners without much more preparation, and there isn't the same great disappointment when a student doesn't show up—someone is always there. Also, the fun and learning with group activities or games often override any extra work, and grouping students of similar abilities makes lesson planning easier. However, there is the need to keep a separate folder for each student in order to evaluate individual progress. Once a group spirit is attained, the students seem to become independent more quickly. They learn from each other. The tutor is not the only source for learning the new language.

Sometimes the question of adding new members to an established group comes up, especially if some members have dropped out. It could be stimulating, but the group members must consider whether or not they want new members. If the group has attained a closeness that has encouraged growth, they might hesitate to invite a new person. Consideration must be given to the level of English (speaking and understanding as well as reading and writing) of the group and of the new student, as well as how the new student's personality would fit with the group. Each group must decide for itself.

In a small group, there will be times when all members will be working together—on a special project, discussing specific topics, or learning something new. But there should also be times when students are working individually or in pairs. It is up to the tutor to plan lessons that are varied, that insure rich interaction, and that build in comfort so that every student will be able to work up to capacity.

Experience has shown that having a husband and wife in the same group is sometimes unwise. When this is a problem, it may be best to place spouses and children in different groups or to match family members with individual tutors.

One-to-One

Traditionally, ESOL tutors in LVA and other volunteer programs have taught on a one-to-one basis. This format has many advantages.

Many new tutors are hesitant to try teaching more than one student. It can be a bit overwhelming, particularly since no two students are at exactly the same level. With only one student, the tutor does not feel restricted to a rigid time schedule because the time and day of the teaching session can be adjusted by a simple phone call.

Many students are more comfortable when they have their own private teacher. They feel their lessons can be more individualized and the pace can be adjusted to their needs and abilities. The time and place of teaching can be adapted to the needs of both tutor and student.

Many ESOL students are so embarrassed by their limited English that they are frightened to enter a class or even a small group. But they are willing to face a teacher in a one-to-one arrangement, knowing that there will be no competition and their lessons will be kept confidential. If ESOL students understand or speak little or no English, they will probably need individual help. In these cases, a one-to-one match may be best. If program resources are available, many students profit by a combination of one-to-one and small group instruction.

COLLABORATIVE LEARNING

One school of thought contends that we learn from each other in our interactions. We can refine our thinking best by discussing with others, reading what others have written, and listening to what others say. We learn and communicate by sharing as social beings. This is the essence of collaborative learning.

Collaborative learning can take place with one student and one tutor working together as well as in small groups where students learn both from each other and from the teacher. The teacher facilitates learning but also learns as part of the group. In either setting, you will learn to set mutually determined goals, negotiating what happens in lessons. Both students and tutors teach and learn during the tutoring process. They share not only English but also perceptions as they mutually expand their social worlds.

Collaborative teaching means that you and your student or students are a team working together for a common purpose. Ideally your students have stated their goals and needs, and you have assessed their skills. They will have many things in common, but you will find differences, too—such as backgrounds, interests, abilities, and time available for home assignments. Together, you can work out plans to help your students attain their goals.

GROUP BEHAVIOR

As you work together, you will find that your relationships with your students are changing. You are trying to make your students more independent of you while building bridges into new learning.

Whether you work with one student or with five, you are a group. Only when you work independently are you alone. Consider five stages in group behavior as suggested by Tuckman and Jensen (1977).

1. *Forming-* As the group forms, the students expect the tutor to take the lead in planning lessons, setting goals, and setting up rules for the group.

2. *Storming-* As individuals within the group grow more independent, there might be resistance to the tutor taking total leadership. They may question the value of some of the techniques and materials. This indicates growth and shows that it is time for students to assume more responsibilities.

3. *Norming-* As a group works closely together, a sense of cooperation and a greater sense of unity usually develop. Individual personalities emerge, and decision-making by the students becomes more evident. They become less dependent on the tutor for guidance.

4. *Performing-* Lessons have become more relaxed, with tutors and students accepting each other, working together, and taking responsibility for decision making. There is a sense of accomplishment and satisfaction as skills of speaking, listening and understanding, reading, and writing are integrated into meaningful tasks.

5. *Adjourning-* Eventually the tutoring must end. Adjourning should not be done abruptly. Time should be allowed for affirmations, for sadness at parting, and for closure. Perhaps a final celebration session can be planned where certificates are given or students share their best work over the year. Perhaps the students will want to plan a final meeting over lunch or coffee. Parting will be easier for the students if they know they can continue to call their tutor and each other for help or encouragement, or just to keep in touch.

It is important to keep in mind that the stages identified by Tuckman and Jensen are only a model. Although actual group dynamics are usually more complex than the model suggests, the stages sensitize us to the ideal of a group's evolution, which can help guide our work.

SUMMARY

Whether you work in a small group or in a one-to-one setting, you will want to be sensitive to your own preferred teaching styles and your students' varied learning styles. Be mindful of differences in dialects and accents as you focus on speech patterns, using authentic materials whenever possible. Working collaboratively, you will be aware of the growth of your partnership or group, as your students progress toward the attainment of goals.

Literacy Volunteers of America, Inc.

ASSESSMENT

CHAPTER

VI

CHAPTER VI
ASSESSMENT

Assessment is the process of collecting and reviewing information about individual students, giving you and the students a basis on which to evaluate their progress and the quality of their work. To be effective, assessment must be linked to instruction as well as function as a measurement of student progress.

Whatever information may be needed for administrative purposes, it is critical that assessment reflect the needs, learning goals, and progress of students. Whatever their backgrounds, whatever abilities or weaknesses are evident, you must be sensitive to each individual's actual learning needs and development. Effective assessment always enhances and guides a student-centered instruction program.

BACKGROUND INFORMATION

Before you start teaching, you should have information on your student's background. This information is usually collected during an intake interview with the student prior to his or her being matched with a tutor. A sample LVA Student Intake Form is shown in Appendix I.

Categories of ESOL Students

People who come for help with learning English can be divided generally into four groups:

GROUP A. Those adults who cannot understand, speak, read, or write any English and are illiterate in their native languages.

Tai Doan and Huong Nguyen came to America as refugees and were adopted by a local social services agency. They were peasant farmers in Vietnam, having lost their homes during the war. They were taken by relief agencies to central camps before coming to America for refuge. Neither Tai Doan nor Huong Nguyen has ever been to school, and neither can read or write in Vietnamese. They know no English.

Those adults in Group A, who are illiterate in their native language and who understand or speak no English, are often the most difficult to teach English. Some argue that these groups of students would learn English more quickly if they were taught to read and write in their native language first, especially if the native language is based on the Roman alphabet. On the other hand, if the native language uses characters and reads from right to left, some of the skills needed to learn to read and write in their native language may not necessarily be useful in learning how to read and write in English. Adults need to decide whether they want to learn to read in their own language before learning to communicate in English. Native-language literacy programs may be available, but you must respect the wishes of your students, who may or may not wish to participate in them.

GROUP B. Those adults who cannot understand, speak, read, or write any English, but who are literate in their own language. They may have anywhere from a few to many years of formal education in their own language.

1. Those students whose language is written in the Roman alphabet, such as French, German, or Spanish.

Ramón is 35 and was born in Saõ Paulo, Brazil. His father was a bricklayer of moderate means, and Ramón attended high school taught in the Portuguese language. Although English is completely foreign to him, Portuguese uses the Roman alphabet, as does English.

2. Those students whose written language does not use the Roman alphabet, such as Hindi, Arabic, or Chinese.

Prakash Singh is from Jaipur, India, and cannot understand, speak, or write English. He is not married and was a clerk in a bank in India. He came to America to join his two brothers, who have started an Indian restaurant. He graduated from middle school in Jaipur, having had all his education in Hindi. Hindi does not use the Roman alphabet.

Some GROUP B students may learn rapidly, but many feel they must learn the way they were taught in school. They want to translate, and they often want to take notes in their native language. This might be helpful, but care should be taken that they do not depend entirely on their written notes since they may never learn to hear or understand the oral language. Exercises and lessons stressing listening skills can be helpful.

Claire Essi came from Syria to a small city in New York state as an 18-year-old bride in an arranged marriage. She graduated from high school and speaks, reads, and writes French as well as Arabic. She can communicate with her new husband and his family in Arabic, but she cannot understand or speak English and wants to be in contact with other young Americans. An early pregnancy made her more anxious to learn English. Her inclination in her tutoring sessions was to write anything she learned in Arabic. Encouraging her to listen, paraphrase, and later write notes in English helped her with conversational English as well as writing.

GROUP C. Those adults who can read and write English at an advanced level, but whose understanding of oral English and speaking ability is limited.

Wei Li had advanced degrees in engineering from Heilongjiang University in the People's Republic of China. He had studied English for eight years and read and wrote it well enough to pass the necessary tests to be enrolled in an American university. However, he had problems understanding the lectures in class and was hesitant to leave his dormitory for fear of getting lost. He found that Americans did not understand his English when he asked for directions, and he could not understand their answers.

Many students have studied English in their own countries for more than ten years. They may have received a good score on the TOEFL (the Test of English as a Foreign Language) or a similar test, been admitted to American universities, and be able to read and write technical materials at the undergraduate or graduate level. However, they still have great difficulty understanding their lectures and the Americans they encounter in everyday living. They feel inadequate speaking English and are hesitant to try, for they have found that most English-speakers cannot understand them. Having Group C students listen to language tapes, radio and TV programs, and your own voice, and having them paraphrase what they hear, while difficult for them, helps to address their specific needs.

GROUP D. Those adults who can understand, speak, read, and write English reasonably well but with some limited proficiency and who have asked for help to improve their English skills.

Vo Tuny, 27, is from Vietnam. He learned some English in the refugee camps. Vo Tuny can read and write English, and he can speak and understand enough English to get by, but he wants help with pronunciation and idioms.

Many ESOL students are in Groups C or D. They can understand and speak some English, but they have trouble with colloquialisms and idioms. They often have sentence structure and pronunciation problems, making it difficult for others to understand them. Their limited mastery of English often restricts achievement of their goals. Those in Group D can often read and write English fairly well, but when questioned, they may say that they do not understand everything they read. Comprehension of English is a problem. It is up to you to help them with their needs as you individualize their lessons. Keeping new words, sentences, and concepts in the general sequence of listening/understanding, speaking, reading, and writing will help many students improve their English. Keep in mind that there will always be a mixing and matching of the communication channels of listening, speaking, reading, and writing. Be prepared to stay flexible.

There are other students who understand and speak English well but have problems reading and writing it. These students should be referred to basic literacy classes. ESOL need not be emphasized in these cases.

Whichever group your students fit into, you must always remember to find out their interests and needs. Tailor your lessons to their goals.

One Russian carpenter was unable to continue his trade in the United States even though he was in an area where there was much building. He didn't know the names of the tools, he could not describe them in English, nor could he understand the details of the job when they were in English. His needs in English would be different, for example, from those of a stay-at-home mom.

Many students in Groups C and D need English for Occupational or Specific Purposes (ESP) or what has been called Vocational ESOL (VESOL).

INFORMAL ASSESSMENT TOOLS

As with all teaching, you do not want to start too far above or too far below your students' levels of ability. How do you determine whether individual students speak and understand little English, are fairly independent in the use of English, or are somewhere in between? A first meeting with your students will help give a general assessment of their abilities and interests, but as you continue your meetings, you will be able to assess areas of your students' growth that sometimes are not evident using informal observation and analysis. There are a variety of published instruments to help teachers assess their students' needs.

English as a Second Language Oral Assessment (ESLOA)

LVA suggests using the *ESLOA (English as a Second Language Oral Assessment)*, by Shaffer and McLean (1996), to help you develop individual student profiles. This instrument measures the amount of English already known and defines areas where help is needed. The *ESLOA* is an example of program-based assessment and is an alternative to more formalized standardized tests.

Description

The *ESLOA* is divided into four progressive levels that indicate aural comprehension and oral proficiency in English. Administration of the assessment is discontinued when the learner cannot satisfactorily complete the required number of items within a level. A training audiotape is available to help tutors practice assessing the fluency, comprehension, and pronunciation of individual students by listening to samples of actual students from various countries.

Level 1 assesses the student's auditory comprehension and does not require an oral response.

Level 2 assesses the student's ability to create language using basic vocabulary and grammatical structures. Short oral responses are required. The focus is on comprehension and meaningful communication.

Level 3 assesses the student's ability to create language using more complex grammatical structures. The focus remains on communicating meaning and on comprehension.

Level 4 is an informal oral interview designed to assess a sample of the student's language. The focus of this section is directed toward comprehension, fluency, and pronunciation.

The *ESLOA* also includes the following:

- ***Tutor Choice*** items, which allow tutors to select items that closely reflect a student's background and interest

- ***Level Description Grid,*** which helps tutors determine a student's ability and shows progress in the categories of general listening, speaking, reading, and writing

- ***Suggested Topics for Life Competencies,*** such as basic skills, community resources, shopping, employment, health, housing, and transportation

Teaching Plans Indicated by Assessment Results

The results of the *ESLOA* will provide valuable information for the development of learner-centered lesson plans appropriate for your students. Here are some suggestions for lessons when working with students at each of the four levels. Keep in mind that content should always be geared toward students' interests and needs.

Level 1 Work on basic conversational English listening and speaking skills, as directed in this book. You can reinforce words the students have heard, understood, and spoken by showing those words in print, but keep written words to a minimum.

Level 2 Work mainly on conversational English (listening and speaking skills), but include reading and writing, beginning with those words, phrases, and sentences that the students can already understand and repeat.

Levels 3 and 4 Advanced students will probably need help with pronunciation, understanding everyday—and possibly technical—English (radio broadcasts, lectures, or meetings, where many people are speaking). All the material that the students have heard, understood, and spoken can be readily introduced as reading material. Students should be encouraged to write, paraphrasing what they've read. Independent reading can be used as a basis for discussion, and independent writing should be encouraged in the form of journals, letters, and stories.

Unless your students speak English quite well, you can assume they will want and need help with speaking and understanding. If their real needs are learning to improve their reading and writing in English, you can use the techniques suggested in this book, but for more help you might want to read LVA's *TUTOR: A Collaborative Approach to Literacy Instruction* (Cheatham, Colvin, Laminack, 1993) or take the basic literacy workshop given by LVA.

ESLOA Level Description Grid

After you have worked with your students even for a short time, you will be able to assess their skills in various areas. The *ESLOA: Level Description Grid* is a practical tool for assessing these skills. You will probably note that most learners do not progress evenly in each category. Some pick up reading quickly, while their conversational skills lag behind. For others, the reverse is true. This is not unusual. It is your job to help your students improve the skills that are most important to them. Most students want to be able to understand and speak English easily, even though these skills are often difficult for them.

ESLOA: Level Description Grid

	General	Listening	Speaking	Work	Reading	Writing
Beginner	Students enter the beginning level with little or no ability to read or write English. Low beginners are unable to function in a situation requiring spoken English. Students at high beginning level function in a limited way speaking English in situations related to their immediate needs.	Students are able to comprehend a range of high-frequency words used in context. Students understand a limited number of very simple learned phrases, spoken slowly with frequent repetitions.	Students can communicate survival needs using very simple learned phrases and sentences. Students ask and respond to simple questions and have some control over basic grammar.	Students can handle only very routine entry-level jobs that do not require oral communication and in which all tasks can be easily demonstrated. Students at high-beginning level can use only the most basic oral communication skills on a nontechnical level.	Students are able to attain limited meaning from print materials with successive rereading and checking.	Students are able to copy isolated words and phrases and generate short sentences based on previously learned material.
Intermediate	Students who enter the low-intermediate level function satisfactorily in the use of English in basic survival situations related to their needs. At the high-intermediate level students can use English to function independently in most familiar situations.	Students comprehend conversations containing some unfamiliar vocabulary. Students understand simple learned phrases easily and some new phrases containing familiar vocabulary.	Students have some ability to participate in face-to-face conversations on topics beyond their survival needs. They clarify meaning by asking questions or simply rewording. Students have some control of basic grammar.	Students can function independently in their jobs, handling job training and work situations that involve oral communication skills on both a nontechnical and technical level. Written directions and materials may need to be simplified or clarified orally.	Students can read simplified material on familiar subjects and have limited success when attempting to read some authentic materials.	Students can generate simple sequential paragraphs related to survival skills, personal topics, and non-personal topics with some errors.
Advanced	Students enter the advanced level with the ability to use English to function effectively in familiar and unfamiliar social situations and familiar work situations. High level advanced students use English to meet most routine social and work-related demands with confidence, though not without instances of hesitation.	Students can comprehend abstract topics presented in familiar contexts. They can also understand descriptive and factual material in narrative form.	Students are able to participate in casual and extended conversation. They communicate on the phone on familiar subjects, clarify general meaning, and control of basic grammar is evident.	Students can meet most work demands with confidence. They can also function effectively in work situations that require interaction with the public. They can follow written instructions in technical work manuals.	Students can read authentic materials on abstract topics in familiar contexts as well as descriptions and narrations of factual material.	Students can write descriptions, short essays, summaries, letters and can complete complex forms or applications. Students can use basic self-correction techniques.

The *ESLOA: Level Description Grid* gives the gradations within each skill so that you can better pinpoint the degree of ability in each area. Make multiple copies of this chart so that each student not only has his or her own chart but a second and third chart to show progress. Circle the box within each category into which you think your student fits. The levels will probably vary from skill to skill. Date the chart, keeping a copy in the student's portfolio. Remember, this is an informal measurement, meant mainly to help you plan lessons to fit individual needs.

Try to assess each student within the first week or two of your work together. You might want to reassess at specific intervals, perhaps every month or two. Show the chart to the students, discussing together which skills are most important to them. Sharing the charts over a period of time gives students visual evidence of their progress and can help them focus on areas that need work without getting discouraged.

Speech Samples

Morley (1991b) suggests that three types of pronunciation assessment—diagnostic evaluation, ongoing evaluation, and actual performance—should be included in the complete assessment of ESOL students. Two kinds of speech samples should be taped early in the teaching sessions:

1. oral reading of a standardized script that incorporates as many features of English pronunciation as possible

2. free speech—encourage free speech by asking open-ended questions

These samples can then be compared to recent assessment tapes to help students note their progress and to identify areas where more practice is needed.

Portfolios

A good way to provide continuous assessment of your students' needs is to keep individual portfolios, or working folders, for your students. Personal information on each student as well as samples of their work, your own notes, the student's progress charts, and your personal assessment after each teaching session may be included. While most portfolios contain written work, include samples of speech using the tape recorder, if possible. Many students want to keep their own portfolios and are willing to make self-evaluations. You may want to make copies of all information so that both of you can have a copy. Be sure that all the student's work includes the student's name and is dated so that progress can be tracked.

Individual portfolios may include

- personal information: name, address, telephone number
- record of student's attendance

- tutor's notes of student's needs and interests
- student's long-term and short-term goals
- *ESLOA* scores and *Level Description Grid* results
- tutor's notes on student's strengths and weaknesses
- taped language experience stories
- taped recordings of student's speaking exercises
- checklist of TV, radio, and movies watched
- writing samples
- student's self-evaluation
- student's personal word list

Besides showing students' progress, portfolios can also include areas that need special attention. For example, some students may be having trouble pronouncing certain sounds in English such as */th/, /ch/, /sh/*. This difficulty may or may not obstruct communication. If you can understand these students, and if others in the group can understand them, it is probably not important at an early stage to address this problem. Make a note of it, and include appropriate pronunciation exercises later on. Other students may bring in idioms that they have heard and don't understand. That should alert you to specific needs and goals. Your notes in individual student portfolios should help you with lesson planning.

You might want to include in your lesson plans a set time, perhaps every two to three months, to review the contents of individual portfolios with your students. Together, you can decide which writing and taped samples to keep and which to remove. These review sessions can be exciting because students often haven't realized what concrete progress they've made.

OTHER ASSESSMENT TOOLS

There are several tools to test the listening, speaking, reading, and writing ability of ESOL students: *Basic English Skills Test (BEST),* the *Comprehensive English Language Test (CELT),* the *Michigan Test of Oral Proficiency, the Test of English as a Foreign Language (TOEFL),* the *NYSPLACE, and* the *ACTFL (American Council on the Teaching of Foreign Languages) Proficiency Guidelines.* Some are administered by institutions at set times; others may be administered by individuals after they have received special training.

SUMMARY

Because the needs and backgrounds of students are so varied, using a range of assessment and evaluation tools is important. It is helpful to have available not only program-based assessment tools, such as *ESLOA,* but also other informal assessment tools, such as speech samples and portfolios. These tools will help you with lesson planning as well as give you and your students tangible evidence of progress.

TECHNIQUES, EXERCISES, AND ACTIVITIES USED IN TEACHING ESOL

CHAPTER

VII

- ♦ COMMUNICATIVE APPROACH

- ♦ LISTENING/ UNDERSTANDING AND SPEAKING

- ♦ SEQUENTIAL/ BALANCED FORMULA

- ♦ READING AND WRITING

- ♦ SUMMARY

CHAPTER VII

TECHNIQUES, EXERCISES, AND ACTIVITIES USED IN TEACHING ESOL

COMMUNICATIVE APPROACH

In this book we suggest using the Communicative Approach for teaching adults with limited English-speaking proficiency, focusing on comprehension and using authentic situations and materials that are representative of everyday life where practical communication is needed. This approach focuses on listening and speaking and is balanced by reading and writing.

The Communicative Approach is an effective and practical way to help adults learn a new language. Students will be able to understand some words in the new language immediately. They will be able to speak some words and sentences, using practical communication skills within the first few lessons. By reading the same words they have heard and spoken, and writing those words, they can reinforce their oral/aural learning. Separating reading and writing from listening and speaking simply fragments language.

The Communicative Approach is learner-centered and learner-directed, allowing students to set their own goals. It stresses the language needed and sought by the students, and gives opportunities for individualized lessons. Students are encouraged to participate in all aspects of the lessons. Because all four skills are taught (listening, speaking, reading, and writing), students can work from their own learning styles while being exposed to other learning and teaching styles. The goal is communication: students should be able to understand what they hear, speak so that others understand them, read with comprehension, and express themselves on paper.

In the Communicative Approach, the emphasis is on communication in real-life situations. But how do you help your students communicate? If your students can speak and understand some English, ask them what they need to communicate. Then pick appropriate exercises to help fill those needs. Sometimes they may have difficulty expressing what they want to learn. You may have to rely on pictures and charades, and you will need to rely on your general knowledge and life experience, at least initially, to guide their learning.

Most of the "tried and true" ESOL techniques, exercises, drills, and other activities can be used by adapting the subject matter to the practical vocabulary your students want. When generic vocabulary is used in an example, tutors can

55

use the concept demonstrated and adapt the vocabulary to what is applicable to individual students. Start simply, but always adapt each exercise to individual goals. To help you understand the various techniques suggested, they will be described separately. In your lessons, you will mix and match techniques, being careful not to overuse any particular one. Rely on your judgment and concentrate on those techniques that work best for individual students.

Although drills and exercises are important, they should not be used in isolation, but rather in real-life simulations using everyday language. The focus is on meaning and communication. As much as possible, draw from real-life contexts for language exercises and drills, and use these as a springboard to stimulate authentic communication. The goal is to transfer knowledge gained from drills and other activities to the students' everyday lives.

There are many positive aspects to drill work. Drill work facilitates better pronunciation, encourages automatic verbal responses, and fosters more confidence in verbal expression. Yet it is important not to overemphasize drill work by making textbook exercises the main portion of the lesson or by failing to link them to real-world communication. Drill work should be viewed as a tool, enabling students to move from controlled to less controlled to increasingly useful communication.

LISTENING/UNDERSTANDING AND SPEAKING

If most people spend an average of 45 percent of their communication time listening and 30 percent of their communication time speaking (see Chapter II), much teaching time should be given to these two areas.

> *We were working in China, trying to learn as much as we could about the people, their customs and daily lives. We also had to "survive," that is, go from one place to another, buy supplies from local markets, order in a restaurant, find the ladies' and men's rooms—all the things we take for granted when we can speak the language.*

> *I cannot write Chinese. I cannot read Chinese. I cannot speak Chinese. I cannot understand Chinese. If I could have a choice of only one of the above four, which would I choose? I would choose to be able to understand what was said around me. Some people tried to be helpful, seeing we were foreigners in distress, and how I wished I could have understood what they were saying! A close second choice would be to be able to speak Chinese so that I could ask questions and respond to their instructions. Of course, I wanted to be able to read the Chinese street signs, the billboards, and the bus schedule so that I could be more independent. But I could survive without being able to read and write. It was very difficult even to "get by" without understanding and speaking any Chinese.*

Listening and Understanding English (Reception)

As suggested above, listening is a primary source of learning for those who want to master a new language, followed closely by speaking. There are several ways for students to practice listening skills. They can listen to complete English sentences, reacting to them in such a way as to demonstrate an understanding of what they heard. New words can be added to their listening vocabulary as quickly or as slowly as is appropriate for individual students.

> *A Japanese woman stated that she had learned to read and write English in Japan. She felt she had a wonderful base for grammar and correct usage of English. But she didn't understand when English was spoken. She felt inadequate when trying to speak English, knowing from people's quizzical looks that they didn't understand her. She said that she'd go to American movies, even in Japan, and wouldn't look at the subtitles. She tried to listen, but she had a difficult time understanding. She often went to the same movie three times, and by the third time, she could understand most of what was said. She admitted that she only knew English* **"through her eyes"**. *She wanted to learn English* **"through her ears"**.

Many ESOL students have suggested that while they can understand their teacher, they have problems understanding other people. Using slower, more precise English is helpful to beginning and intermediate learners, but our goal is to help students comprehend the English that is spoken by natives, which is usually at a faster pace, full of contractions and with the words run together. Thus, we must be careful not to speak too slowly or enunciate more clearly than we usually do.

Even beginning ESOL learners profit by listening to a variety of native-speakers to get the rhythm of the language. Even though they can't understand all the words, they'll get the feel of the language. Listening activities should be included in each lesson. Exposure to a variety of listening exercises is important. For a listening activity, students can be asked to

- listen and recognize
- listen and identify
- listen and select
- listen and complete a task

The task could be drawing a picture, following directions on a map, or opening a book to a specific page.

When working with students who know little or no English, an effective way to assure listening comprehension is through Total Physical Response (TPR). Oral commands or directions can be given, demonstrated by the tutor, with physical responses expected from the students. No oral responses expected; the responses are the actions of the students. When students perform appropriately, you know that they understand. You might say:

Pick up a blue pencil. (You might want to add *please,* but be sure your students don't confuse *please* with the command given.)

If the students pick up a blue pencil, you know they understood.

Another practical and easy method of teaching, listening, understanding, and speaking is to use pieces of colored paper as examples of following oral directions. This is an excellent exercise for students who understand or speak no or very limited English. A detailed description of the specific steps as adapted from Gattegno's *The Silent Way* (1963) is included in listening/understanding activities in Chapter VIII (see "Colored Paper Exercises").

Gestures/Commands/Questions

You may want to establish some useful gestures needed for nonverbal communication with your students.

- *Listen-* Often students repeat whatever you say. If you want them only to listen, you can indicate for them to be quiet and listen by cupping your hand next to your ear, putting your finger on your lips and saying, *Listen* or *Shh!*

- *Respond-* If you want your students to imitate you or respond or answer a question, open your hand, palm up, toward the students.

- *Repeat-* When you want your students to repeat what you said, point to the students and use the charade gesture meaning *Come on* (hand open, palm up, fingers moving).

- *Tutor responds-* When you expect to respond yourself, point to yourself as you start talking.

- *Speak together-* When you want your students to say something with you, point one hand at yourself and gesture with the other hand in a circular motion to include all your students, as in charades.

For beginning ESOL students, it's important to start simply. Use a command, directing the students to act (as in TPR). At first use simple commands, demonstrating as you speak. For example, *Stand up.* Repeat the command and gesture to your student to stand up. Then move to *Sit down.* Again, demonstrate and suggest the desired response. Then, *Walk, Stop,* and *Turn around.* The tutor walks, stops, and turns around to demonstrate. You can add more vocabulary when you feel it is appropriate (e.g., *Take one step. Take two steps. Open the door. Close the door.*).

When your students understand, demonstrating by their actions, you can give the appropriate gesture for them to repeat the commands. They can take turns telling you or other members of the small group what they want you or others to do. They are already in the leadership role, deciding what they want done. Even at this beginning stage, collaborative teaching is taking place—the tutor is not the only one giving directions.

After the students have understood and have said the words, the tutor can write them on a piece of paper or a blackboard. The tutor reads the words first, then asks the students to read and then write them.

Continue with some more commands, giving the appropriate demonstrations, expecting only a physical response, no words. Commands such as *Point to . . . , Touch . . . ,* or *Pick up . . .* could be combined with *the door, the table, the book, your nose, your head*, or even *the red book.* As students master commands, add other verbs, such as *open, close, give, take,* etc. It is only after the students have demonstrated that they understand the words by appropriate actions that you will ask them to repeat the words, then read them, and finally write them. You might want to include other commands and questions which the students can use in their daily lives, e.g., *Where is the . . . ? Show me the. . How much . . . ? May I have . . . ?*

COMMANDS Directing Your Student to Action		
Stand up. Sit down. Walk.		Turn around. Stop.
Point to	the door. the table. the window.	the floor. the book. the pen.
Touch		your nose. your finger. your hand. your head.
Pick up		the book. the red book. the black book. the green book.

The substituted words should keep to the same pattern, with only one word or phrase changing at a time.

Point to the door.

Point to the table.

Point to the pencil.

Vary the commands along with the vocabulary only when your student is more advanced.

> *Pick up the yellow pencil.*
>
> *Stand by the window.*
>
> *Turn off the lights.*

When your students understand and can repeat these commands, give them opportunities to read and write those same words. You might want to label the items or the pictures.

This same exercise can incorporate vocabulary specifically needed for individual students. If the student is a hairdresser, you might have him bring in objects used in the beauty salon: comb, brush, hair dryer. If the student is a carpenter, appropriate objects might be a screwdriver, a wrench, a saw, and a hammer.

Telephones/TVs/Radios

Telephone conversations call for advanced listening skills. There are no gestures, no visual contact to help communication. The ears alone must do the work. Practicing telephone calls gives excellent training in both listening and speaking. Enunciating clearly on the phone is especially important. One Spanish-speaking student kept hearing *all of you* as *I love you* during a phone conversation. You can imagine the complications this might create!

One way to help your students learn to listen and speak via telephone is to have two people sit back-to-back, simulating a situation where there is no eye contact. The two people could be you and a student or two students. Have similar objects available to both, e.g. several books, pens, and other objects. Have one student give directions. For example, *Open the red book to page 68 and put a marker on top of the page number. With the black pen, draw a circle and a square at the bottom of the page.* Check to see that the listener has understood enough to do what the speaker asked. Then switch roles.

A next step could be asking your students whom they need or want to call. They can look up the numbers in a telephone book and practice a telephone conversation. The students can suggest the situations—a call to make a doctor's appointment, get a bus schedule, or speak to the tutor. They may require a detailed script at first, then a script with open-ended sections for them to fill in. Finally, an ad-lib conversation would provide a follow-up and model for the real event. You and your students or two students could role-play.

Secretary: Dr. Brown's office. May I help you?
Patient: This is Mr. Malipo. May I make an appointment for Tony, my three-year-old son? He has a bad earache.

Secretary: Can you bring him in this afternoon at three?
Patient: Yes, thank you. We'll be there at three.

Some students who read in their own languages may resist practicing listening skills because they are attuned to written messages. But such students may not be able to understand a conversation or a radio broadcast in English. They know more at eye-level than at ear-level and often insist on seeing the words in print. This may defeat the very purpose of their work with you. Encourage them to listen for comprehension of a word, phrase, or sentence, and then to repeat it, assuring them that you will give them the written version later. Then suggest they try to write the words if that will help them remember, without worrying about spelling them correctly. Then they can compare your words with theirs to see if they heard right and to check their spelling, which they can correct if they wish.

Suggest that difficult lectures or broadcasts be recorded either by you or the students so that they can be listened to as often as necessary. You could suggest that both you and your students listen to the same radio or TV news broadcast and discuss it at a lesson together. By giving your students an opportunity to review what they heard, you have helped develop the thinking skills needed for effective listening as well as for effective reading. For intermediate and advanced students, you might suggest they focus on one news commentator at a time, getting used to that person's pronunciation. In this case, it's helpful to have them read the news headlines in the newspaper *before* they listen to the commentator. This gives them the opportunity to predict the main stories.

Comprehension Checks

Some people can pronounce words in English which they do not understand. Be careful not to assume comprehension simply because the words are said correctly. During a tutoring session, you can often sense that your students do not understand a word you have said—sometimes by a quizzical look, a cock of the head, or raised eyebrows.

An important part of your job in teaching language skills is to assure comprehension of what you say. If you ask, *Do you understand?*, a nod or even a response of *Yes* does not guarantee comprehension. ESOL students are often embarrassed that they do not understand or may want to please you by saying they understand. You can do a real service to your students by suggesting it is certainly proper and polite to say *I don't understand*. However, it is necessary to find other ways to determine to what extent they understand.

One way is to have student action follow a direction:

Please open the window and tell me what you did.

If your student not only opens the window but says, *I opened the window,* then you know the student understood. If the response is, *I open. . . ,* you model the correct response, *I opened the window,* gesturing for the student to repeat the entire sentence.

Yes/No Questions

How you state a question often determines what kind of a response you will get. There are questions where a yes or no response is appropriate.

Is the door closed?

Is the book blue?

Although *Yes* or *No* questions elicit simple responses, students must understand the whole question in order to answer correctly.

Either/Or Questions

Questions can be phrased to allow for alternate answers. For example:

Is the door open or closed?

Is the book red or blue?

With these questions the right answer is contained in the question. In a way, either/or questions are both teaching and checking comprehension at the same time. For example, comparatives can be reviewed using *either/or* questions:

Is it hotter here or in your country?

Does it rain more here or in your country?

Wh- and How Questions

Still other questions demand more language in the answer such as *Wh-* questions *(who, which, where, what, when, and why).* *Wh-* questions use the intonation pattern that rise at the end.

Who is president of the United States?

When was the Constitution of the United States written?

Why do you want to work at that company?

Some questions, such as open-ended questions, are appropriate for advanced students because they require descriptive answers. *How* questions usually require that students state a fact or explain a process. For example:

How do you register your children for school?

How do you get to work?

How is the climate different in your country from the climate here?

Information Gathering

Advanced students can be asked more problem-solving and information-gathering open-ended questions, which demand greater knowledge and require more inference. For example:

If you need a plumber, how would you find one, and how would you determine if he or she was qualified?

The tutor must vary the level of difficulty of the questions in accordance with the ability of the individual student and the nature of the task.

> **Comprehension Checks**
> 1. Action to follow directions.
> 2. Questions.
> 3. Back-to-back session with common directions.

Pictures, actions, and basic question patterns can help ascertain whether or not your students really understand the meaning of both the spoken and written language. Other listening exercises are found in Chapter VIII.

Speaking English (Production)

Language is for communication. The type of language you focus on with your students should be authentic and relevant. It should be authentic in the sense that it is the type of language people actually speak, not textbook English. It should be relevant in that the language relates to your students' needs and interests. It should focus on the things they want and need to communicate. Work with the vocabulary and objects your students know or want to know and those in which they've shown an interest. Keep in mind, though, that your goal is to help your students expand their English communication skills rather than simply to learn isolated vocabulary or decontextualized grammatical rules. Consider the following anecdote:

> *One tutor said that she worked with two people from Peru. They had lived in New York City in a Spanish-speaking community for seven years. They understood English well. They could even read and write English. They tried to speak English, but they told the tutor that people almost never understood them. Their tutor agreed—it was nearly impossible to understand their English. They needed help with stress, rhythm, and intonation patterns as well as with individual sounds.*

Accents that do not interfere with listeners' understanding need not be a problem. Pronunciation differences are only important when they make communication difficult or impossible. New tutors of oral language skills are often overly concerned about correcting students' pronunciation of English words. Unless pronunciation interferes with communication, you should not correct it in the early lessons, perhaps noting the difficulties so that you can work on them later. Don't expect your adult students to overcome a foreign accent easily or completely. Accent elimination in another language is difficult for most adults. However, it is important for them to hear and be able to reproduce sounds effectively if that is their goal. *I spik Inglis* can become *I speak English* with practice.

A child learning to talk is constantly imitating, improvising, and practicing. However, the adult who is learning a new language has one difficulty that the child does not have. The child has no inhibitions about practicing, whereas many adults, fearful of sounding foolish by mispronouncing words, are much more reticent. But even for a child, learning a new language takes time.

Many of us have studied a foreign language at one time or another, but we may not be comfortable speaking with a native speaker of that language. We may become self-conscious and tongue-tied, even though we might be able to read the language quite well. It is up to you as a tutor to establish a comfort level for your students so that they are relaxed enough to try the new sounds and the new words.

In a misguided effort to be understood by newcomers who understand and speak little English, we sometimes chop our sentences short.

> *A woman, trying to be helpful to her Laotian friend who didn't speak English very well, said,* "You here stay. I take baby. I put her down for nap." *The woman believed that she was making it easier for her friend to understand. If she had said,* "You stay here. I'll take the baby and put her down for a nap," *the words would have been just as easy to understand if spoken a bit more slowly than normal but with proper stress and intonation.*

Modeling English

Much of learning a language is a matter of imitation and practice. Your students must hear and understand what is said in a normal tone and at normal speed. What is said can then be repeated and become a regular part of a new English-speaker's discourse.

While nouns and verbs communicate a lot, the major units of meaning in English are in the context of phrases and sentences, not individual words. Therefore, use phrases and sentences as the basis for instruction. Because your students need to understand English as it is spoken in America, your speech becomes an important model they follow. Speak naturally, repeating if necessary to give the students a second or third chance to catch the sounds and intonation. Here are a few do's and don'ts, using the sentence *The woman is walking down the street* as an example:

1. **Don't overarticulate.** Words can become distorted if you over-emphasize certain sounds (e.g., *waa-lking* for *walking, streee-et* for *street*). It is important that when you speak English to your students it is not distorted but represents the language they will hear in normal conversation, unless you are trying to help focus attention on a particular sound. Most people your students hear will not overarticulate except for emphasis (e.g., *I'm sta-arved!* or *Watch out!*).

2. **Don't speak too slowly.** Students who become accustomed to a speaking rate geared to the lowest level will find it difficult to converse or to understand normal speech. *(The woo-man izzz waah-king dow-en the street.)*

3. **Don't speak too loudly.** Speaking loudly does not facilitate understanding. Your students don't have trouble communicating in English because they are hard of hearing. *(THE WOMAN IS WALKING DOWN THE STREET!)*

4. **Do be aware of correct intonation.** The meaning can be changed, for example, if the voice rises at the end of a sentence. This rise indicates that a question is being asked. *(The woman is walking down the street?)*

5. **Do be aware of correct stress.** Avoid the use of unnatural emphasis on certain words. *(The woman is **walking** down the **street**.)* She is not running and is not on the sidewalk.

6. **Do be natural.** Use phrases and contractions as you normally would. *(The woman is walking down the street* or *The woman's walking down the street.)*

In expecting students to repeat what was said with similar speed, stress, and intonation through modeling, many tutors forget to use repetition for more complex activities—to develop grammar structure and expand vocabulary and meaning. We're all natural mimics, so use repetition throughout your lessons, always checking for comprehension. If you model a sentence or a structure and if your students show comprehension of what you have said and repeat it, they will be using listening and speaking skills.

Stress, Rhythm, and Intonation Patterns

In learning a new language, stress, rhythm, and intonation patterns are as important as vocabulary and comprehension.

Stress

Without being conscious of it, native speakers naturally stress some syllables in a word and some words in a phrase or sentence. Stressed syllables or words are usually louder, more clearly enunciated, and longer. Unstressed syllables or words are generally reduced, shorter, and weaker.

> *am* **bi** *tious*

> *de* **vel** *op ment*

Changing the stress on individual words within a sentence can alter the emphasis of meaning. For example:

> *Roberto is sitting on the CHAIR* (not on the sofa or on the floor).

> *ROBERTO is sitting on the chair* (not Luis or Maria).

Sometimes words with the same spellings are pronounced slightly differently with the stress on different syllables. The content will give the clue for pronunciation. For example:

> *The court clerk made a* **record** *of all the testimony.* The first syllable is stressed when the word is used as a noun.

> *She was asked to* **record** *all the testimony.* The second syllable is stressed when the word is used as a verb.

Rhythm

Every language has a rhythm of its own. Hearing English every day in real-life settings or on the radio, TV, or tapes helps learners become familiar with the rhythm of the language.

One way you can help your students hear the rhythm of the English language is by having them tap out the syllables of a sentence you say with a pen on a table or clap out the beat of the rhythm with their hands. After they have tapped through a sentence and repeated it several times, ask them how many taps they made. All the students may not agree on the number of taps in the sentence. That is okay at the beginning of the lesson. Native English-speakers tend to run words together, but the rhythm of the language is based on the sound of the sentence, not necessarily on the actual syllables in the sentence. If the students are having trouble agreeing on the number of syllables in your sentence, slow down a bit so as not to run the words together. This may change the number of syllables they identify at first, but after they have repeated the sentence several times, encourage them to practice natural speaking. Start simply and go to more complex sentences.

> *My name is Alphonse. I'm from Mexico. (10 taps)*

> *I got a telephone call from home. I'm so happy. (13 taps)*

> *Let's go to the supermarket and get some food for dinner. (15 taps)*

Rhythm can be also taught through songs, poems, and choral readings.

Intonation

Intonation refers to pitch changes, often called the melody of a language. Unnatural pitch may interfere with communication. Without correct intonation, a person can't always be understood, no matter how perfect the utterance.

As described in *New Lives in the New World* (1975), Nila Magidoff discovered that it takes more than word knowledge to communicate effectively.

> *Nila arrived in the United States from Russia and was asked to give a speech for the Russian War Relief organization. Her English was limited, but she optimistically said she would do it if they would give her two weeks. Two weeks? To Nila, even two weeks seemed impossible—but she decided she could do it by writing down 50 words every day and learning them phonetically. Every day she learned 50 more words, and every night she prepared a new list of 50 words. To help her pronunciation, she went to the movies and listened to poetry on audiotapes. She had not sought out a tutor because she felt she could move ahead faster on her own. She felt that if she knew the words, people would understand what she said, even though she was sure her speech would have grammatical errors. The big day arrived, and she gave the speech. She felt certain that her efforts had proven effective. What a disappointment it was when one man took her hand and said, "Thank you so much. I didn't understand a word you said, but it was all so beautiful."*

Nila Magidoff learned that the meanings one wishes to communicate require not only knowledge of specific words and correct word order, but appropriate intonation patterns as well.

A world of meaning is expressed through intonation patterns that we most often learn by listening and repeating, not by memorizing rules or specific instructions.

One way to help your students understand and hear the changes in pitch is to say a sentence and convert its intonation pattern into a sing-song pattern. For instance, even a simple question like *Where are you going?* could be converted into *la la la* **la** *la?* with the emphasis on the fourth syllable. Even though your students don't understand the meaning of the sentence, they can hear the rise and fall of the pitch pattern.

Would you please tell me where Highway 80 is?

la la laaa la la la la la **lala** *la?*

In this sentence, *please* is naturally extended, so *laaa* is extended. *80* is naturally emphasized, so *lala* is emphasized. The question mark indicates a rise in pitch. For this exercise, suggest that your students concentrate on the intonation patterns rather than on the words.

The pitch of the native English-speaker's voice naturally rises slightly at the end of questions that require a *yes* or *no* answer *(Will you go to the library with me?)* instead of dropping as it does in a statement. The rise in pitch provides an important cue that you are seeking an answer. If you slow down your speech and overemphasize stress and intonation, natural intonation patterns can become distorted, leaving meaning unclear.

Individual Sounds

ESOL students often have difficulty with certain small muscular movements of speech that are not used in their native language. For the same reason, English-speakers often have similar trouble with some of the guttural sounds in German, the nasal sounds in French, and the clicks in some African languages.

Before students can approximate a sound not found in their native languages, they must hear and recognize that sound when it is contrasted with similar sounds. The sequence of learning requires that the sound be *heard* distinctly, then *identified* so that attention can be focused on it. Don't be discouraged if your students can't hear or produce all English sounds. Remember—understanding their speech is the objective, not perfect diction.

Many students can hear certain words or sounds, and they can repeat the words or sounds, even correcting their own mispronunciations. But for others, hearing and correcting can be very difficult, especially if that particular English sound does not exist in their native language. It is helpful to show your students how to form the sound. For example, if your students cannot make the */th/* sound, suggest they put their tongues between their teeth and give a breath. Demonstrate by making the sound yourself, or give your students a mirror so the students can see the mouth's shape and the tongue's position.

Many words have an entirely different meaning when only one sound is changed. *Sin* is much different in meaning from *seen, tin* from *teen, fill* from *feel*. It is important that students understand that when communication is distorted by mispronunciation, the resulting meaning is often radically changed.

Minimal Pairs

Spanish-speaking students often have difficulty with the English */v/*. Students from other language backgrounds typically have trouble with the */th/* sound. Many Asians confuse */l/* and */r/*. Others have trouble distinguishing */v/* and */b/, /i/* and */ee/, /m/* and */n/, /oo/* and */o/, /eh/* and */ah/*. As a result, certain words will confuse your students because they sound alike to them: *vest* and *best, thin* and *tin, read* and *lead, moon* and *noon, soup* and *soap, letter* and *ladder.* It is your task to help them hear the differences.

You might use minimal pairs, two words that differ in only one sound (e.g., *set* and *sat, bet* and *bat*), to focus on the differences. Select a group of word pairs that provide examples of the same contrast (e.g., the */p/* and */b/*). Use a regular dictionary or a rhyming dictionary if you need help.

pill - bill	*pail - bail*	*pie - buy*	*pay - bay*
pair - bear	*pest - best*	*pat - bat*	*pull - bull*

Try to use familiar words to keep the exercise short yet meaningful. At first, use words that represent concrete items *(pear/bear, pill/bill)*. Occasionally they will not be spelled similarly *(pair, bear)*, but spelling is immaterial for this exercise. It is the sound similarity you are looking for. Keep sets of minimal pairs together at first *(pear/bear, pill/bill)*. Later, mix them up and see if your students can hear the differences *(pear, pill, pull)*.

1. First, you will want your students to hear the difference between */p/* and */b/*. Ask your students to listen as you say each word in each pair. Have them raise one finger when they hear the */p/* sound and two fingers when they hear the */b/* sound. Or you might have them write */p/* and */b/* signs and have the students hold up the appropriate card.

2. Next, you will want your students to produce just one of those two sounds in ifferent words. They will say the words by repeating them after you.

Tutor: pill	**Tutor:** pair	**Tutor:** pail
Student: pill	**Student:** pair	**Student:** pail

Then have your students say the words with the second sound, repeating after you.

Tutor: bill	**Tutor:** bear	**Tutor:** bail
Student: bill	**Student:** bear	**Student:** bail

3. To help your students understand that these small sound differences are important, put the words with contrasting sounds into different sentences and contexts.

Where's the pill? I have to take it now.

Where's the bill? I have to pay it now.

Repeat the first question in each pair above, letting the students give the appropriate follow-up sentence:

Tutor:	Where's the pill?
Student:	I have to take it now.
Tutor:	Where's the bill?
Student:	I have to pay it now.

A correct response indicates that the student can now hear the difference between */p/* and */b/*.

4. Next, reverse the roles. Let the students ask the questions, and you respond. Tell them they can read the questions out of order. If you give the responses they expect, they will know that they are pronouncing the sounds correctly.

Student:	Where's the pill?
Tutor:	I have to take it now.

Student:	Where's the bill?
Tutor:	I have to pay it now.

For home practice, you could write the pairs of words, suggesting that your students practice repeating both words until they can say and hear the differences clearly. But it would be even more helpful to use a tape recorder. You say the paired words on tape, leaving a space so that your students can repeat the words.

Linking

Linking means blending the end of one word into the beginning of the next word so there is no separation. Native speakers of many languages link words all the time. When the last consonant of a word is the same as the first consonant of the following word, we usually pronounce that sound only once, linking the two words.

Call the main number.

Often words that begin with a vowel are linked to a preceding consonant.

I'm eating an apple.

Alert your students to the speech patterns, and give them exercises so that they can hear and say linked words correctly.

Pausing

Native English-speakers speak in "chunks" or thought groupings. In writing, this is often shown with punctuation. Where we pause often determines whether our spoken language is comprehensible or incomprehensible. Note the difference in meaning when pauses fall between different words.

Martin said (pause), *The grocer gave incorrect change.*

Martin (pause), said the grocer (pause), *gave incorrect change.*

One exercise to help your students pause at meaningful times is to write out sentences and put a slash mark (/) where you suggest pausing or taking a breath. You can use slash marks to show pause breaks in simple substitution drills, in dialogues, or wherever they would be helpful. Start with short phrases, then group them together for longer chunks.

Let's walk / to the market / to get vegetables. /
Let's walk / to the library / to get books. /
Let's walk to the market / to get vegetables and fruit. /

You can also use dialogues:

- *Where are you going? /*
- *I'm going / to the garage / to have my car fixed. /*
- *How long / will you be gone? /*
- *About two hours, / so don't wait for me. /*

Another exercise to help students practice pausing is to have them repeat telephone numbers, pausing after the area code and again at the dash.

Contractions and Reduced Expressions

Most English-speakers use contractions in place of full pronouns and verbs (e.g., *isn't* for *is not, he's* for *he is*) and reduced expressions which blend two or more words into one (e.g., *helpim* for *help him, wanna* for *want to*).

Iz'e working?   in place of   *Is he working?*

Do you wanna come along?   in place of   *Do you want to come along?*

It would be a mistake for the tutor, in an effort to teach "correct" English, to avoid the use of contractions, or reduced expressions, or to try to pronounce each word individually and distinctly. In everyday English, your students are more likely to hear *I won't, She's goin,* or *Where d'ya work?* than *I will not, She is going,* or *Where do you work?* Students will need to know that *I'm* means *I am,* but specific knowledge of contractions can be emphasized later. The shorter version may be more immediately useful in speaking, depending on whom the student speaks with most often.

Summary of Pronunciation Issues

Traditionally, teaching of pronunciation has focused on the practice of isolated sounds or words without regard for the context in which those sounds or words occur. In a Communicative Approach, stress, rhythm, intonation, and other aspects of pronunciation must be learned beyond individual sounds or words, since adequate mastery of real-life speech is what is needed to be understood. Phrases and complete sentences, therefore, provide better contexts than isolated words or sounds when helping students learn pronunciation.

Importance of Oral Exercises

Drills are extremely important in facilitating new language acquisition. They provide a structure to reinforce patterns of learning and at the same time allow for improvisation. As the following discussion will demonstrate, drills range from the simple to the complex. In a Communicative Approach, drills should be created from real-life situations so that they can ultimately be used in authentic English-speaking settings.

Simple Substitution Drill

Substitution drills are very useful because they give students a model of correct sentence structure. In a simple substitution drill, you merely substitute one word, leaving the rest of the sentence the same. Be sure your students understand each sentence you say. Use vocabulary that students are familiar with. The point of this exercise is to practice putting words in correct sentence structure. You might start with sentences about objects in the room, pictures in a magazine, or sentences that use action verbs that can be demonstrated. As always, substitute the vocabulary in this exercise with words related to your students' interests. To begin, point to an object and say (gesturing for the students first to listen, then repeat):

It's a chair.	*Point to the motor.*	*Put the baby's diaper in the drawer.*
It's a pencil.	*Point to the tire.*	*Put the baby's blanket in the drawer.*
It's a book.	*Point to the fender.*	*Put the baby's shirt in the drawer.*

Names of objects from students' personal word lists (words they've identified as important) can be used in this drill.

Using this drill, your students can get intensive practice with a single grammatical structure. However, don't be misled into thinking your students can say these sentences independently just because they repeat them easily. Repeat the same sentences several times. Repetition helps build confidence by providing practice of learned material that can then be used in varied contexts.

A word of caution when using the substitution drill: when a new word is substituted in a sentence, it is common to overemphasize that word. If you do this, your students, using you as a model, will do the same thing. For example, using pictures to demonstrate what you are saying, you unintentionally say:

The MAN is running.

The WOMAN is running.

In a normal conversation you probably would not stress *man* or *woman* unless you were comparing the man and the woman. You might stress the word *running*. Therefore, generally, as you substitute words in a structure, be careful to talk with natural stress and intonation.

The man is running.

The woman is running.

In a Total Physical Response activity, be sure that the action corresponds to the sentence. Be sure that both you and your students are seated as you say, *I'm sitting*. Stand up and gesture for the students to stand as you say, *I'm standing*. Start walking and encourage the students to walk as you say, *I'm walking*.

Once the students have learned even a simple speech pattern, show how it can be used again and again by changing just one word, adapting to vocabulary your students want and need. You can make this simple substitution drill more challenging by changing two words instead of one, keeping the structure the same. For example:

It's a green pencil.	*It's a striped shirt.*
It's a red book.	*It's a leather belt.*

SUBSTITUTION DRILL		
I'm	eating. reading. carrying.	
You're They're	carrying	the book. the books.
He's She's I'm We're	reading eating	a newspaper. a recipe. my lunch. our dinner.

This same substitution drill can be used for a more advanced student by showing a picture and first giving the structure, having the students listen, then repeat it. For example:

The family is going to the clinic.

Then give only the word to be substituted: *supermarket, library, school*.

Tutor: The family is going to the clinic.
Student: The family is going to the clinic.

Tutor: supermarket.
Student: The family is going to the supermarket.

Tutor: library.
Student: The family is going to the library.

Tutor: school.
Student: The family is going to the school.

Complex Substitution Drill

Substitution drills are called complex drills when the substituted word(s) go into different slots in the sentence. Students have to think about the meaning of each word as they decide where the word must go.

Tutor: The family is going to the clinic.
Student: The family is going to the clinic.

Tutor: Girl.
Student: The girl is going to the clinic.

Tutor: Walking.
Student: The girl is walking to the clinic.

Tutor: Library.
Student: The girl is walking to the library.

After the students have heard, understood, and spoken the words in the substitution drills, write those same words on paper or the board so that the students can read and write them.

Substitution Drill
Simple

Substitute one word in a sentence, with an appropriate action for comprehension.

"Here's a book."
"Here's a chair."
"Here's my pencil."
"I'm sitting."
"You're sitting."
"We're sitting."

Substitution Drill
Complex

After giving a basic sentence, give only the cue word for substitution.

T — "Mary is walking to school."
S — "Mary is walking to school."
T — "...running"
S — "Mary is running to school."
T — "...work"
S — "Mary is running to work."

Response Drill

An early step toward getting your students to be independent is to work on response drills. Through the previous substitution drill, you have already taught the students statements that could be answers to questions. Through repetition, the students will begin to sense a pattern of the answers which will help them use what they've been practicing in other settings. A start can be made in the tutoring session by having students make statements and ask questions about activities in each others' daily lives using the drills they have been practicing.

For the beginning-level students, actions and pictures will be necessary to supplement the drill. Of course, before you ask the question you must be certain that your students have the information and language practice needed for the appropriate answer. You are not quizzing for facts. You are giving repeated practice in understanding and responding to common questions. Thus, at the beginning levels, your procedure should be to model and teach the answer first, having the students repeat, and then ask the question. Your first activities will be obvious and simple, using any available props (e.g., opening a door, walking around a table). Afterward, let students suggest activities.

Tutor:	I'm eating dinner.
Student:	I'm eating dinner.
Tutor:	What are you doing?
Student:	I'm eating dinner.

After several repetitions, reverse the procedure. Suggest that the students ask you or each other the questions.

Be careful not to ask questions beyond your students' comprehension. Build on words the students already know and help them learn to say words and sentences commonly used in ordinary conversation.

Tutor:	I'm studying English.
Student:	I'm studying English.
Tutor:	What are you studying?
Student:	I'm studying English.

When you have taught a basic structure, such as *I'm going to the library. Where are you going?,* you can suggest putting different words in the same slot by showing different pictures.

Tutor:	I'm going to the library.
Student:	I'm going to the library.

Tutor:	(shows picture of a post office) Where are you going?
Student:	I'm going to the post office.
Tutor:	(shows picture of a supermarket) Where are you going?
Student:	I'm going to the supermarket.

Variations of the response drill are endless. You could include a real or imaginary visit (using pictures) to the grocery store to shop for food and teach the students the various ways items are sold, e.g., by the pound, by the loaf, by the dozen.

Tutor:	I'd like a dozen rolls.
Student:	I'd like a dozen rolls.
Tutor:	I'd like a loaf of bread.
Student:	I'd like a loaf of bread.
Tutor:	I'd like a pound of cheese.
Student:	I'd like a pound of cheese.

Using appropriate pictures, the question and answer would be:

Tutor:	What would you like?
Student:	I'd like a dozen rolls, a loaf of bread, and a pound of cheese.

Notice that you are actually combining the response drill with a substitution drill.

Early in the teaching sequence you might want to help students become familiar with the names of various types of appliances or pieces of furniture in the home. You can draw stick figures or cut out pictures from magazines to help as you use the response and substitution drills.

Use pictures to elicit a variety of responses. Eventually you won't have to model the response; it will come naturally. The length of time this will take will depend on the picture, the vocabulary, and the student. When you show pictures to your students, this question could be answered simply or with a detailed reply:

Tutor:	What's this man doing?
Student:	He's fishing.
	or
	He's trying to catch fish, but he'll have a hard time because he doesn't have a net.
Student:	He's walking.
	or
	He's walking to work, carrying a newspaper.
Student:	He's running.
	or
	He's running to catch the bus.

Questions about pictures often give your students a chance to provide a wide range of responses. As you ask the question *What's the girl doing?* you might expect the answer *The girl is sitting,* but one student may say, *The girl is smiling,* and another may say, *The girl's playing.* You have helped them use acquired vocabulary independently. Encourage creativity. Creativity fosters learning and is fun.

Creating their own questions are important milestones for students. They will need to learn to ask questions for which they will need the answers. They will need to be able to understand a practical response as well. During a tutoring session you can ask what language needs your students had that week and incorporate them into the lesson.

> **Student:**   Where do I get the bus for Main Street?
> **Tutor:**   Go to the next corner. The bus comes every ten minutes.

You can always end each exercise by writing the words and sentences used, giving the students the opportunity to read and write the words and sentences. As your students advance, start asking questions for which you haven't already given the answers. This exercise requires real thought and leads to authentic communication.

Response Drill

The tutor holds a picture of a girl in a boat.

T — The girl is in the boat.
S — The girl is in the boat.
T — Where is the girl?
S — The girl is in the boat.

Transformation Drill

In the transformation drill, students

- change positive statements to negative statements and, conversely, negative statements to positive statements

- change statements to questions and questions to statements

Prepare the students for changing a positive statement into a negative one by having them repeat both the positive and negative sentences after you. Pictures or quickly drawn stick figures may help with comprehension.

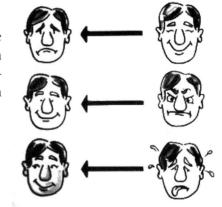

| **Tutor:** | The man is happy. |
| **Student:** | The man is happy. |

Shake your head as you say,

| **Tutor:** | The man is not happy. |
| **Student:** | The man is not happy. |

After students have had sufficient practice with both positive and negative sentences and understand the pattern, continue with a more complex transformation drill, supplying the cue word *not*.

Tutor:	The man is happy.	or	The man's happy.
Student:	The man is happy.	or	The man's happy.
Tutor:	Not.		
Student:	The man is not happy.	or	The man isn't happy.

As students understand the positive/negative transformation, you might want to teach how some negatives do not merely add the word *not* but actually change the wording a bit. As you show a picture of a boy holding a dog, you could say:

Tutor:	Jimmy has a dog.
Student:	Jimmy has a dog.
Tutor:	(cover dog with your hand) Not.
Student:	Jimmy does not have a dog.

or

Jimmy doesn't have a dog.

Question patterns may be more difficult. When changing statements to questions, you can cue the students by holding up a card with a question mark on it. You may have to teach the ? symbol.

```
┌─────────────────────────────────────────┐
│          Transformation Drill             │
│          Positive to Negative             │
│  (pointing to pen)                        │
│  T — "This is a pen."                     │
│  S — "This is a pen."                     │
│  (pointing to book and shaking head)      │
│  T — "This is not a pen."                 │
│  S — "This is not a pen."                 │
│  For more advanced students               │
│  (show picture of bus)                    │
│  T — "This is a bus."                     │
│  S — "This is a bus."                     │
│  (show picture of motorcycle)             │
│  T — "not"                                │
│  S — "This is not a bus."                 │
└─────────────────────────────────────────┘
```

Model the sentence, having the students repeat it. Then restate it in question form as you hold up a card showing a question mark.

Tutor: Harry is going to work.
                or
             Harry's going to work.

Student: Harry is going to work.
                or
             Harry's going to work.

Tutor (holding ? card): Is Harry going to work?
Student: Is Harry going to work?

Model several sentences in this way. Then try giving a statement, holding the ? cue card.

Tutor: Marie is reading a book.
                or
             Marie's reading a book. (Hold ? card as cue.)
Student: Is Marie reading a book?

As students start to understand changing statements to questions, you might say:

Tutor: Ask me if I'm going home after class.
Student: Are you going home after class?

Tutor: Ask Mary where you can find the bus schedule.
Student: Mary, where can I find the bus schedule?

Transformation drills can also be useful when teaching harder concepts, such as irregular past tense verbs (*see/saw, come/came, go/went, am/was, think/thought*). These exercises, too, can be reinforced by having the students read, then write the words they have been practicing orally.

Backward Buildup

Often a sentence is just too long for students to repeat it correctly the first time. They may have no problem at the beginning but have trouble near the end. Backward buildup provides practice in repeating long sentences with more practice at the end where the problems are. By maintaining the same intonation patterns and repeating each phrase, your students will be consistently hearing those same patterns.

In the following sentence, *We're going to the supermarket to buy meat and vegetables for dinner,* students can often repeat the first two phrases correctly, but stumble on the third and usually can't remember the fourth.

First divide the sentence into phrases:

We're going / to the supermarket / to buy meat and vegetables / for dinner.

1	2	3	4
Okay	Okay	problem	problem

Say the sentence as a whole. Then begin the backward buildup. Start on the last phrase, proceeding forward from there. Use a natural stress and intonation pattern for each fragment.

Tutor:	For dinner.
Student:	For dinner.
Tutor:	To buy meat and vegetables for dinner.
Student:	To buy meat and vegetables for dinner.
Tutor:	To the supermarket to buy meat and vegetables for dinner.
Student:	To the supermarket to buy meat and vegetables for dinner.
Tutor:	We're going to the supermarket to buy meat and vegetables for dinner.
Student:	We're going to the supermarket to buy meat and vegetables for dinner.

Thus, there is more repetition of the phrases that cause the most problems. As usual, follow up the oral practice by allowing the students to read and then write these same sentences.

Because you can speak and understand English, these sentences give you no trouble. If you were trying to say them in a foreign language, however, you'd probably struggle, too. To empathize with the difficulty your students experience, try the following technique with a friend, using numbers. Use three numbers to equal one English phrase. Have your friend say the entire sentence (three sets of number phrases) at a normal speed.

Friend: 425-346-2917
You: 425-346 (probably)

If this is too easy, try it with four or more sets of numbers. No matter how many sets of numbers are used, this exercise illustrates the difficulty that students learning a new language face.

The backward buildup technique helps students remember phrases long enough to put them all together:

Tutor, then Student: 2917

Tutor, then Student: 346-2917

Tutor, then Student: 425-346-2917

This technique can be used with lower-level students who have trouble with shorter sentences, but it is particularly helpful as your students are expected to repeat longer and longer sentences.

Backward Buildup

If your conversational English student has trouble repeating a complete sentence as modeled by the tutor, start the drill by using the *last phrase of the sentence.*

*He went/ to work/ at six o'clock/
on Tuesday morning./*

T — "...on Tuesday morning."
S — "...on Tuesday morning."
T — "...at six o'clock on Tuesday morning."
S — "...at six o'clock on Tuesday morning."
T — "...to work at six o'clock on Tuesday morning."
S — "...to work at six o'clock on Tuesday morning."
T — "He went to work at six o'clock on Tuesday morning."
S — "He went to work at six o'clock on Tuesday morning."

Literacy Volunteers of America, Inc.

Chain Drill

A chain drill is a good way to have people in a small group introduce themselves. It's easy yet informative. To begin, sit with your students around a table, or arrange your chairs in a circle. You could start by saying:

My name is . . .

Turn to your neighbor at your right or left and say:

What's your name?

That person responds with his or her name and asks the same question of the next person.

This continues around the circle.

The repetition is simple enough so that even a shy, beginning level student can participate and gain confidence. The chain drill can be expanded to other statements and questions. Always give your statement first as a model and then ask a question:

I'm from New York State. Where are you from?

I'm from Puerto Rico. Where are you from?

If your students are from different countries, you might have a globe or a large map available, giving students an opportunity to pinpoint their countries.

You can add other questions, each time varying the chain drill a bit:

I've lived in Middletown for twenty years. How long have you lived in Middletown?

I drove my car to school. How did you get here?

I have two children and six grandchildren. Do you have a family?

I like to play golf and ski. What do you like to do?

I took a walk last night. What did you do last night?

Another chain drill activity is for the students to make up a narrative based on a picture, an activity, or an experience. Each student adds one phrase or one sentence to the story and must repeat all the preceding phrases or sentences. Exactly the same wording is not necessary; paraphrasing is perfectly acceptable. For example:

Tutor:	When Maria first came to America, she. . .
First Student:	When Maria first came to America, she didn't have a friend.
Second Student:	When Maria came to America at first, she didn't have friends or a teacher.

One variation would be to have each student add a sentence or short paragraph that continues a story without repeating the parts that came before. Such improvisation is especially useful with advanced students in helping them to discover and expand the range of their mastery of English.

Tutor:	The Gómez family decided to go on a picnic.
First Student:	They wanted to see the big lake they had heard about.
Second Student:	But first they had to get food to bring.

Even with beginning students, you can use chain drills to give practice in understanding and saying confusing individual sounds. Have pictures available of objects whose names begin with the confusing sounds. For example, if the confusing sounds are /v/ and /b/, have pictures of vegetables, vitamins, vanilla, and vinegar, and beets, bananas, broccoli, and bread. Have the students choose pictures and substitute the words shown in their pictures in the appropriate place, adding more words.

We went to the market and got vegetables and bread.

We went to the market and got vitamins, vegetables, bananas, and bread.

Chain drills help students relax and have fun at the beginning of lessons while also giving practice in listening and speaking.

Creative Exercises

There are an infinite number of exercises that allow students to use language creatively. A few of these exercises follow.

Sentence Combining

Giving your students an opportunity to create more complex sentence structures from simple sentences can help students with independent speaking.

Tutor:	This coffee is hot. This coffee is strong.
Student:	This coffee is hot. This coffee is strong.

Gesture by bringing two hands together to suggest combining the sentences as you say:

Tutor:	This coffee is hot and strong.
Student:	This coffee is hot and strong.

Your students will get the idea and respond with new examples.

Tutor:	The truck is large. The truck is expensive.

Literacy Volunteers of America, Inc.

If you gesture to combine those sentences, students will probably say:

Student: The truck is large and expensive.

Teach additional connecting words such as *but, so, when, before, after, then,* and *because*. Write each word on an index card. Let the students choose a card. Say two sentences that can be combined with the connecting word they picked.

Tutor: The building is five stories high. It is difficult to walk to the top floor.

Student: The building is five stories high, so it is difficult to walk to the top floor.

Tutor: I burned my tongue. I drank hot coffee.

Student: I burned my tongue because I drank hot coffee.

Sentence Combining

1. Tutor says two short sentences.
    T — The coffee is hot.
        The coffee is strong.

2. Student repeats.
    S — The coffee is hot.
        The coffee is strong.

3. Tutor gestures to combine them and says,
    T — The coffee is hot and strong.

4. Student repeats.
    S — The coffee is hot and strong.

Once this routine is comfortable for the student, use only steps 5 and 6. If this becomes difficult, return to steps 1 through 4 also.

5. Tutor models,
    T — "The coffee is hot. The coffee is strong."
        gesturing to combine.

6. Student says,
    S — "The coffee is hot and strong."

Restatement

As students become more proficient in speaking English, you can have them restate specific sentences, putting the information in the first person singular.

Tutor: Tell me that you are going to the library.
Student: I'm going to the library.

Substitute various phrases to reinforce the concept.

Tutor: Tell me that you are looking for a book.
Student: I'm looking for a book.

Tutor: Tell me that you are reading stories to your children in English.
Student: I'm reading stories to my children in English.

This is an effective way of encouraging your students to talk without their simply repeating what you say.

Another way to restate is to suggest that the students ask the tutor questions.

Tutor: Ask me where I went on my vacation.
Student: Where did you go on your vacation?

Tutor: I went to Arizona on my vacation.

You can ask advanced students to restate longer and more complicated sentences. They must remember the original sentence, creating new words and ideas on their own.

Restatement

Ask the students to restate a sentence, putting it in different words.

Tutor: Tell me that you are enjoying your vacation.
Student: I'm enjoying my vacation.

Giving cue words (e.g., *today, yesterday, tomorrow*), have your students restate a sentence using appropriate verb tenses.

Tutor: Today I'm riding the bus to work.
Tutor: Yesterday . . .
Student: Yesterday I rode the bus to work.

Tutor: Tomorrow . . .
Student: Tomorrow I'll ride the bus to work.

Tutor: Last week I saw an accident and got a call today to be a witness.
Student: You saw an accident last week, and today you got a call to be a witness.

Again, for advanced students more difficult structures can be used. You can teach the tenses without using the terms *present, past, future* by modeling and then restating them with the appropriate adverbs (e.g., *today, yesterday, tomorrow*).

Tutor:	Today I am (I'm) having lunch with a friend.
Student:	Today I am (I'm) having lunch with a friend.
Tutor:	Yesterday I had lunch with a friend.
Student:	Yesterday I had lunch with a friend.
Tutor:	Tomorrow I will (I'll) have lunch with a friend.
Student:	Tomorrow I will (I'll) have lunch with a friend.

When the students have practiced and understand how the cue words *today, yesterday, tomorrow* indicate a change in tense, first give a sentence and then only the cue word.

Tutor:	Today I'm playing tennis.
Tutor:	Yesterday . . .
Student:	Yesterday I played tennis.
Tutor:	Tomorrow . . .
Student:	Tomorrow I will play tennis.

Completion

Your students can get additional practice in forming correct sentences and a chance to be creative by completing sentences that you start. You can use pictures to suggest the new vocabulary or you can leave it to your students' imagination.

Tutor:	I went shopping and bought . . .
Student:	I went shopping and bought six oranges.

If you have several students in your group, you could have each add one item (a chain drill), having each student repeat the items suggested before.

Student:	I went shopping and bought six oranges and two apples.

If you are working with advanced students, they may want to make more complicated additions.

Tutor:	On the way to class . . .
Student:	On the way to class, I met two men from my country, and we had a nice talk.

Continuing Story

To encourage advanced students to speak spontaneously, use the Continuing Story exercise. The tutor starts the story, setting the stage and giving the students an idea of what is expected. To help the person continue the story, allow for a range of options by leaving the final sentence unfinished. The student can add one or as many appropriate sentences as he or she can. The tutor can continue the story, or, in a small group, a second student can add to the story.

Completion Drill

The tutor begins a sentence suggesting the student complete it appropriately.

T — "I have..."
S — "I have a new car."

Tutor:	I know an old man. He lives . . .
First Student:	He lives across the street from us and is known to everyone. He enjoys watching the children. He is . . .
Second Student:	He is very poor, but he brings cookies every day to share with the children. One day . . .
Third Student:	One day the old man wasn't in his usual place on the park bench. The children missed him and wondered what happened.

This story could go on and on, with the tutor and students continuing to add their own ideas, creating a mystery, a charming short story, a love story—whatever they want.

What follows is an example of a more advanced continuing story in which both the tutor and students are expected to give longer responses:

Tutor: The bus came up the street. It was the #20 bus, just the one I was looking for. We had formed a line, and I was in the middle. The man in front of me reached into his pocket and pulled out . . .

This gives the next person an opportunity to say whatever comes to mind, not taking too much time to think. The students can take more time thinking as the story develops, but encourage each student to stop in midsentence. Each student must speak, trying to be creative in using the English he or she knows. At the end of the lesson, suggest that the students write the story in their own words, then read the story to their group.

The exercises suggested can be used with beginning as well as advanced students. Introduce them simply, repeating them often until the students understand the concept and see the pattern. Repetition may seem boring to you, but it builds confidence and gives needed practice to the students. It is a long road between saying something once and having it come naturally in a conversation.

TECHNIQUES, EXERCISES, AND ACTIVITIES USED IN TEACHING ESOL

Continuing Story

1. Tutor starts the conversation.

   Tutor: I bought a used car The color is . . .

2. Each student adds as many appropriate sentences as he wishes.

   Student: The color is blue. It's a 1982 Ford, four door. I got an
                  excellent deal and it's in good . . .

   Student: It's in good shape. Yesterday as I stopped for a red light,
                  the car in back of me . . .

3. Continue as long as it is of interest to the students.

4. Each student writes her own version of the story.

5. Each student reads her story to the group.

Dialogue

A dialogue is a conversational exchange between two or more people in a given situation. An effective way to present and practice the patterns and structures of English is through dialogue rather than in isolation. Try to tie the dialogue to the topic of the lesson if possible. You can incorporate all the techniques presented so far: substitution drill, response drill, transformation drill, chain drill, and backward buildup.

Memorized dialogues are especially useful with beginning students. Free dialogues spring from a topic the students are familiar with, and are built with vocabulary and structures the students know.

Memorized Dialogue

A dialogue to be memorized can be taken from an ESOL text, or you can prepare it yourself. You can help your students memorize the dialogue through repetition and response drills. Even at a basic level, dialogues can and should resemble brief, real-life conversations. Together, decide on the topic to be used in the dialogue. Be sure to use pictures or props if your students need them to understand. Keep the sentences simple and limited to four lines at first. A sample for a beginning student might be:

Tutor:	Would you like a cup of coffee?
Student:	Yes, thank you.
Tutor:	Sugar and cream?
Student:	No, I take mine black.

An advanced student could memorize a more complex dialogue.

Gesture for your student to listen, or say, *Listen*. First, say the entire dialogue, performing any activities or using any objects or pictures to aid understanding. By sitting in opposite chairs or by turning your head a different way for each person, the tutor indicates he or she is one person for lines one and three and another person for lines two and four. You can also use cards with names indicating speaker A or B. Or you can use pictures of two people from a magazine as the imaginary dialogue partners.

When modeling the dialogue, be sure to speak as you would speak normally. Talk with normal speed and rhythm. Speak clearly but not too loudly.

- Present the entire dialogue at least twice before you ask the students to repeat it.

- Break it down by sentences. Say the first sentence. Ask your students to repeat it several times until you feel they can say it with fairly good pronunciation. Then do the same for the second sentence, sitting in the opposing seat or showing appropriate actions. Repeat this process for each line. You may have to repeat each line several times before your students are comfortable with them.

- Repeat the entire dialogue. This time, act it out, having your students listen.

- Say each line together. Go through the dialogue, having your students say each line with you. Repeat several times until your students have the dialogue memorized. Be sure your students understand the meaning of the dialogue. Next is the performance.

- You say the first line, your students responding with the second line. Continue this pattern line by line until the students can say their lines readily.

- Reverse the roles, having the students say the odd-numbered lines while you say the even-numbered lines. If you have a small group, you might divide the students into pairs to have them practice the dialogue.

- When the pattern is learned, you can substitute words such as *tea* for *coffee* or adapt the dialogue in some other way, keeping the same general pattern.

Tutor:	Will you have a sandwich?
Student:	Yes, thank you.
Tutor:	Tuna salad or ham and cheese?
Student:	I'd like ham and cheese.

Use pictures to cue the students to give more than one likely response, using substitution drills.

Taping dialogues for review at home is helpful. As students repeat the sentences with the tape recorder, they get practice with pronunciation as well as with the normal rhythm of the language. If you have more than one student, you will have to repeat the dialogue enough times to record it for each student. Or, if you have a dual-cassette tape player, you can spend a few minutes after class copying the master for each student who brought a blank audiotape.

For advanced students, use more complex dialogues. Dialogues provide a safe setting for students to practice talking about a subject without having to rely on their spontaneity. For the following dialogue, bring pictures of a refrigerator, cheese, meat, and bread to the tutoring session. The tutor points to the appropriate pictures and gestures for the students to listen and then repeat the dialogue.

Second Speaker:	What's in the refrigerator? I'm hungry.
Second Speaker:	There's cheese, meat, and bread. Why don't you make a sandwich?
First Speaker:	Yes, that sounds good.
Second Speaker:	Why don't you make one for me, too?
	or
	Would you make one for me, too?
Second Speaker:	All right, I will.
	or
	Okay, I will.
	or
	Sure.

With every dialogue, go through all the steps as suggested. In the following dialogue, perhaps the students couldn't repeat the second line. This is a perfect time for backward buildup.

Tutor:	A sandwich.
Student:	A sandwich.
Tutor:	Why don't you make a sandwich?
Student:	Why don't you make a sandwich?

Tutor:	Meat and bread. Why don't you make a sandwich?
Student:	Meat and bread. Why don't you make a sandwich?
Tutor:	There's cheese, meat, and bread. Why don't you make a sandwich?
Student:	There's cheese, meat, and bread. Why don't you make a sandwich?

Using pictures, you can change the situation. Instead of a refrigerator, a picture of a cooler or picnic basket could be used. Other food can be substituted in the dialogue. Eventually the students will feel confident enough to adapt the language learned in dialogues to other situations.

After you and your students have gone through a dialogue, suggest that your students copy the dialogue onto a piece of paper for home study; if they have difficulty with writing, give them a copy to read at home. You might suggest that they practice the memorized dialogue with a tape recorder for home practice. They can refer to the printed dialogue if they wish.

One of the most difficult things for tutors to realize is that language must be overlearned. Language learning requires a lot of constant review and repetition. "Once over lightly" simply will not suffice. Remember, everything is new, and much repetition is needed to build confidence as well as new vocabulary.

Dialogues are worth all the effort of practice. The rewards come when they lead to real conversation.

Free Dialogue

Conversing spontaneously in real-life conversations is the primary goal of most ESOL students. Prepared or cued dialogues can provide an entrance into free dialogue or discussion. Action pictures as well as student-suggested situations can be starting points for free dialogue.

Dialogue

Dialogue is a conversational exchange between two people. Incorporate all the techniques as they are needed. Keep the dialogue simple at first and keep it to four lines.

1 — "What's this?"
    2 — "It's an orange."
1 — "Do you like oranges?"
    2 — "Yes, oranges are good."

       Steps for learning dialogue
1. Tutor says entire dialogue, being sure the student understands content/meaning.
2. Tutor says first sentence.
   Student repeats first sentence.
3. Tutor says each sentence
   Student repeats each sentence.
4. Tutor says entire dialogue
   Student listens.
5. Tutor and student say together the entire dialogue.
6. Dialogue: Tutor
         Student
         Tutor
         Student
7. Reverse the roles if appropriate.
8. Variations for further practice: substitute words or lines, especially on the tutor's part; add new lines for a longer dialogue; combine two, short related dialogues.

An entertaining way to use free dialogue is to take a sequence of cartoons and cut out the words. Using the situation in the cartoon as the basis for a dialogue, you and your students decide what words you would like the characters in the cartoon to say. It is desirable to stimulate free dialogue as soon as possible, recognizing that with beginning-level English-speakers the amount of discussion will be minimal compared to more advanced speakers of English.

Role-playing is an important tool for introducing and practicing free dialogue. As a group, pick a situation for a role-play and then act out a dialogue. Perhaps your students will be visiting a school soon. You could pretend to be the office receptionist. In character, ask your visitors questions. Your students should respond. You might want to tape the entire dialogue, playing it back so that the students can hear themselves.

Ask your students to suggest some of the situations where they need help: in stores, in pharmacies, in banks, at doctor's appointments, on the bus, or at work. Act out as many dialogues as seem useful based on these and other relevant situations. Have the students break up into pairs when feasible. Possible scenarios for them to enact could be cashier and customer, pharmacist and customer, bank teller and customer, nurse or doctor and patient, bus driver and passenger, or supervisor and employee.

Dialogues help students to practice using English in real-life situations. Write lots of dialogues for your students. Write simple dialogues of your own or suggest that your students write dialogues for the situations listed below or others they identify.

- using the phone to make an appointment
- using the phone in an emergency or to tell the tutor that there has been an unexpected event and the lesson has to be rescheduled
- talking to a doctor, nurse, or pharmacist
- ordering food in a restaurant
- asking directions
- returning an item to a store
- asking the landlord to repair something in the apartment
- seeking information about work
- enrolling a child in school
- making change

Idioms

An idiom is a succession of words whose meaning is not obvious through knowledge of the individual words, but must be learned as a whole (e.g., *give way, in order to, be hard put to, run up the bill*).

In his book, *Doctor of the Barrios (1970),* Dr. Juan Flavier said that when he was trying to know the people of the Philippines better so that he could teach them English, he found that it was just as important to know their idioms as to know their more formal language. He gave this example:

One day a farmer asked him if he wanted "kisses honey." He declined because he wasn't sure what was meant. His colleague accepted and the farmer opened an old biscuit tin. It contained shredded tobacco and cigarette paper. Then the meaning became clear. The farmer put some tobacco on the rectangular paper, rolled it expertly, and licked the edge to keep it in place.

Hence, *kisses honey* was a hand-rolled cigarette.

American idioms are just as difficult and just as confusing for the person trying to learn American English. Yet idioms are accepted as part of everyday speech. They cannot be translated directly, and their meanings are not always easy to explain.

He's broke.

Give me a ring.

My new car was a real steal.

I'll drop you a line.

Idioms should be taught, giving explanations of their meanings as they are repeated.

He's broke. He has no money. He's broke.

Provide several explanatory sentences so that your students can understand the meaning of the expression and become comfortable with it. Even though English-speakers understand the meaning of many idioms, it is often not easy to explain them to someone else. There are many books on idioms which could help you. Also, ask students to bring to class idioms that they would like to discuss.

Sentence Structure/Grammar

When thinking of the structure of the English language, most of us do not analyze why we say something a certain way. We say it the way we do because it sounds right. For example, we wouldn't say, *I to work go,* but rather, *I go to work.* We wouldn't say, *This pencil not is sharp,* or *This pencil not sharp is.* We'd say, *This pencil is not sharp.*

Even those of us who have studied formal English grammar do not always know which rules we follow when we speak, but we generally know implicitly what is right. Your aim as a tutor is not primarily to teach grammatical rules but standard usage so that your students will get a feel for the accepted form of spoken English.

Literacy Volunteers of America, Inc.

After a while, grammatically correct sentences will begin to sound right to your students, and you can avoid teaching many confusing rules about language and grammar. Often a student will want to know why something is said in a certain way, but avoid talking about the rules of grammar to your students unless they specifically ask. Instead, teach correct usage by practicing with properly structured phrases and sentences. If they do ask, avoid lengthy, technical explanations.

In teaching sentence structure, you should be aware that proper word order is essential for accurate communication in the English language and that the same words can convey a totally different meaning when their order in a sentence is changed. For example, every native English-speaker knows that although identical vocabulary is used in these two sentences, they describe two totally different experiences:

The dog bit the man.

The man bit the dog.

With beginning students, use sentences that can be illustrated during your tutoring session. Of course, whenever possible, use vocabulary relevant to your students' lives.

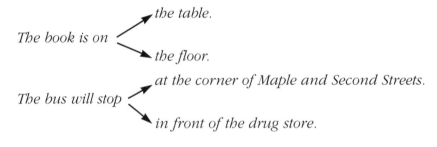

At times you may want to prepare simple grammar checks for the students by having them decide which of two sentences is correct according to the picture.

For simple grammar contrasts (singular vs. plural; male vs. female, now vs. everyday), prepare several sentences. Say them and have the students indicate which category each fits into.

Tutor:	He's swimming.
Student:	Now.
Tutor:	He eats at Big Burger.
Student:	Every day.
Tutor:	They work at the factory.
Student:	Every day.
Tutor:	They're riding the bus.
Student:	Now.

If your students want detailed help with English grammar, there are many books available (see annotated bibliography). Be selective with textbook activities so as not to overdo isolated drill work. It is important for students to have sufficient practice with correct grammar, especially if they ask for it, but the goal of language learning is effective usage rather than memorization of rules. You and your students need to work out the proper balance between structured grammatical exercises and free conversation, which will differ depending on students' educational backgrounds, learning styles, and purposes for learning English.

Expanding Vocabulary

For real competence in English, your students will need an ever-expanding vocabulary. Instead of having the students memorize vocabulary lists, introduce new words within known structures or within similar word group meanings. Substitute new words in sentences and patterns you are already working on. Be sure your students understand their meanings by using actions, objects, pictures, questions, or a bilingual dictionary. When introducing new vocabulary words, talk about their stress patterns as well as their meanings.

New Vocabulary within Known Structures

Instead of having students memorize words in lists or in isolation, put the words in sentences and use pictures. For example, if the words to be learned are *coat, hat,* and *tie,* you could use a simple substitution drill, putting the new words in sentences:

He's wearing a coat.

He's wearing a hat.

He's wearing a tie.

If the words are more difficult to understand, such as *beautiful* or *fading,* you could use pictures or a bilingual dictionary to depict the meaning. Always present the new words in sentences.

Writing down new words is helpful. You or your students might want to write labels that they can post on objects around their homes or at their workplaces. Encourage your students to bring in pictures or descriptions of objects for which they want the English words. This is a good way to start developing personal word lists.

New Vocabulary within Word Groupings

When teaching new vocabulary, it is helpful to teach words in groupings and in context:

- words associated with particular situations, such as *doctor, clinic* and *medicine* or *act, acting,* and *actor*

- words illustrated by pictures or objects at hand, such as *table, chair, purse,* or *door*

- words which are related to everyday needs, such as days of the week, months, numbers, colors, parts of the body, or shopping list items

Vocabulary that relates to the students' needs and interests is always more effective than abstract vocabulary. Illustrate the new word in a sentence to teach the meaning rather than simply giving a definition. Meaning will usually come by associating the new word with other English words they already know:

A person who works for a company is an employee.

The person who hires him is his employer.

A person who has a job is employed.

After your students have heard these new words, understood their meaning, and repeated them, they should read them and finally write them down.

Word Cards

All learners want to see progress. One concrete way ESOL students measure progress is by increasing the number of vocabulary words they know. To help them increase their vocabularies, have your students put each vocabulary word on a 3" x 5" index card or a quartered card. If the student can say the word, recall its meaning, and use it correctly in a sentence on three separate occasions, then they probably know that word.

Put one check mark on the index card if a student says a new word correctly without having heard it modeled (from picture, action, and so on).

refrigerator ✔

stove ✔

Put another check mark if a student says the word correctly at a second lesson.

dishwasher ✔✔

silverware ✔✔

Put a third check mark if a student says the words correctly at a third lesson. By then one can assume that the student knows the word. Be sure, though, that the student knows the meaning of the word and can use it correctly in a sentence as well.

toaster ✔✔✔

Students often feel they are not learning new English words fast enough, and a pile of these cards shows graphically how many new words they are learning. These cards can be reviewed for home study.

When students can use the new vocabulary words to create new, original sentences, you can be assured that they are growing toward independent speech.

Importance of Practicing Listening and Speaking Skills

Even native English-speakers do not always understand what is said to them. Perhaps the listener wasn't paying attention, or there was background noise; maybe the speaker didn't speak clearly or with proper stress and intonation. Establish with your students some appropriate ways to communicate lack of understanding (e.g., *Could you repeat that, please? Excuse me? Pardon? I didn't understand what you said.*). Practice these and other similar expressions with your students. Your students will find these expressions very useful as they are developing their speaking and listening skills.

Students might want to structure their learning more by setting aside some time each day, or even a whole day each week, with their family when only English is spoken.

> *While working with a young English teacher in China, I found that her dream was to have her two-year-old son speak English. In China all adults work, so the grandparents, if they are retired, are often responsible for raising young children. This woman's parents only spoke Chinese, so she wondered how she could help her son. She admitted that at the end of a busy day, neither she nor her husband (who also spoke English) felt like communicating in English. I suggested that perhaps they'd want to set aside just one hour a day—perhaps an hour in the morning or an hour right after dinner—when only English was spoken. Since her son's primary caregivers spoke no English, the only way her son was going to get enough exposure to English to eventually pick it up was if she and her husband spoke English around him on a regular basis.*

SEQUENTIAL/BALANCED FORMULA

The sequential/balanced formula is suggested when presenting new material to students who particularly want help with listening and speaking skills balanced with reading and writing. This formula is helpful to students who read and write English fairly well but have difficulty understanding and speaking English. This can be a model for the tutor to follow as a guide.

LISTEN	1. Tell or read aloud any story or other new material of interest to the students (simple, medium, or advanced, depending on the listening level of students), motioning for or asking the students to listen. Don't give them a copy of the text. Use pictures, props, and gestures to aid comprehension. Read one paragraph at a time unless you are sure the students can comprehend more.
	2. After each segment or paragraph, review any new vocabulary, explaining the meanings of unknown words to the students if they cannot guess them from the contextual clues.

SPEAK

3. Read the same paragraph aloud again, this time sentence by sentence or phrase by phrase, as a model for pronunciation, having the students repeat aloud each phrase or sentence. Before reading, it is helpful to make slash marks in the text where you would naturally pause.

4. Ask individual students to tell in their own words what they heard you read aloud. This is called paraphrasing.

5. Continue the above procedure, segment by segment or paragraph by paragraph, to the end of the text.

6. Give the students a copy of the same material you read aloud. Ask them to read the passage silently to themselves.

READ

7. Ask one student at a time to read aloud. Adults are often asked to read aloud to a group—instructions from a manual, stories to children, or passages during a religious meeting. Reading aloud during the lesson helps build confidence and is a good way to check pronunciation.

SPEAK

8. Discussion: For the intermediate or advanced students, ask questions and ask for opinions. Examples of critical-thinking questions are *Why do you think the author said . . . ?* or *What do you think would have happened if* (change the story) *. . . ?*

WRITE

9. Homework: Have the students paraphrase the story in writing. This will give you the opportunity to check grammar, spelling, and punctuation for future tutoring sessions focused on writing issues. It will also give you a sense of your students' writing fluency and style.

10. Respond: positively to written homework. All English lessons should include all four language skills for new material: listening, speaking, reading, writing. If you don't have enough time in one session to cover all four skills, you should review what was done in the previous session and move on to the skills you omitted last time.

Nyeng, a beginning-level ESOL student from Vietnam, was hesitant to shop at the huge supermarket. She wanted to know how to ask where items were and how much they cost. Her tutor read a prepared dialogue asking the appropriate questions and giving answers. Nyeng repeated, then paraphrased the dialogue. She couldn't read, so that skill had to be skipped for the present, but the written dialogue became the text for her beginning reading and writing lessons.

• • •

Two young men, Level II (beginner-intermediate level) in ESLOA, (Mikael from Latvia and Bong from Vietnam), were craftsmen at a local furniture factory. They had been given a manual to read on the care of expensive tools. Their supervisor was going to question them on its contents. They asked their tutor to help them understand the material. When their tutor suggested they might want to write a summary of the manual, they were excited but overwhelmed. They thought they could never do it.

Their tutor read aloud paragraph by paragraph from the manual, asking questions and having them paraphrase what she had read. After all, they knew more about these expensive tools than the tutor did. Together they wrote key words on the board. From the key words they had a good discussion on the contents of each chapter. Even though their reading was at a low level, their tutor gave them copies of the manual to read as best they could. Then she had each write, using the key words as an outline, a short summary of the manual. They were hesitant but tried. Their ability to understand and talk about the material surpassed their reading and writing skills. But they did get their thoughts on paper—and, after a bit of editing, they were delighted to share their knowledge with their supervisor.

• • •

Four young mothers, Level IV (advanced level) in ESLOA (Ruo from China, Tatiana from Russia, SunHwa from Korea, and Christine from Brazil), wanted to be able to go to PTA meetings and neighborhood group meetings and be able to understand what was being said. Often several people spoke at the same time, and they spoke rapidly. The women could understand written material but had problems understanding spoken English, especially if it was in the form of a lecture or speech. They found their common interest was family life and values in the United States.

Focusing on their common interest, the tutor read a short article about family life in the United States in the mid-1990s. She brought in information on family life in the early 1900s and they had a discussion comparing the two eras. She had asked them to jot down key words or phrases, highlighting the material read and discussed.

They worked on new vocabulary words, questioning and paraphrasing, and had a lively discussion, which was interspersed with information on family life in each woman's native country. The tutor suggested that each one write a short report on family life and values in the United States, using their key words as a guide. Their initial objective was to get their ideas on paper, not to focus on grammar, structure, or spelling.

At the next session, each student read her paper aloud to the group. The others listened, then added their own ideas or asked clarifying questions.

It gave the tutor an opportunity to check pronunciation, grammar, etc. Each student edited her own paper, then asked the tutor to edit it. After a final edit, the tutor typed their papers. They took great pride in the project, knowing they had listened with comprehension; discussed, questioned, and paraphrased; taken individual notes; and written reports. They effectively presented and edited their own reports, using language skills in a project that was invaluable to these young mothers.

Adjust the order of the various communication skills to the needs and learning style of individual students. Be sure to include all the skills—if not in a single lesson, then in your general working plan with your students.

SEQUENTIAL/BALANCED FORMULA
1. Learners hear and understand English spoken, read, or taped.
2. Learners repeat the same English sentences or story. (optional)
3. Learners paraphrase aloud what they heard.
4. Learners read the same material.
5. Learners write in their own words what they heard, said, and read.

READING AND WRITING

While all the techniques that have been discussed in this book up to now stress listening and speaking and are reinforced immediately by reading and writing, you will also need to know specific techniques and approaches for teaching reading and writing in English to those who do not know how, including some who are literate in their own language.

For students who know little or no English, reading will probably be limited to the lesson material. Be aware that there are signs or labels that your students must read daily. Include them in your lessons. Thus, reading street signs (e.g., *STOP, EXIT, EMERGENCY*), labels on medicine bottles (e.g., *take one tablet twice a day*), ladies' and men's room signs, etc., should be taught early.

Manuscript/Cursive Writing

Even the most basic ESOL students must be able to say their names and addresses, as well as read and write them. Teach your students to write in manuscript (print) first because it most closely resembles the writing they will read. Books, magazines, or anything typed will be in manuscript. Signs, labels, and job applications are other examples of text that use manuscript. Cursive writing (script) should probably be taught after your students are fairly comfortable with printing.

However, some adults will want to write in cursive early. If so, teach them the alphabet in cursive and explain when it is appropriate to use it. You might want to practice your own manuscript and cursive writing to make sure your students can read your writing. Models for the manuscript and cursive alphabets are in the appendix. Even students who cannot write in their own languages don't necessarily need to begin by writing the alphabet. They can learn letters by copying the letters in their names or in words they need to know.

Determine Your Students' Current Level

Chapter VI included an extensive discussion of the levels of ESOL students. What follows is a short review.

Group A:- Students cannot understand English and are illiterate in native language.

Group B:- Students cannot understand English but can read and write in native language.

      1. Native language—Roman alphabet
      2. Native language—non-Roman alphabet

Group C:- Students can read and write English but have limited speaking and understanding skills.

Group D:- Students can read, write, speak, and understand English, but with limited proficiency.

After a few sessions with your students, you should be able to identify the level for each student. Knowing the backgrounds, abilities, and goals of your students will help you determine how much to stress independent reading and writing.

For students who write with Roman letters, writing in English will come more easily. But for students whose native language uses non-Roman letters, reading and writing English may be more difficult. For students who cannot write in their own language, you may have to start at the most basic levels—even holding a pen in their hands may be new to them.

Techniques for Teaching Reading and Writing

Your students want to learn to read and write English independently, and you can help them acquire these skills. Skills are important but comprehension is the heart of language learning. Little is accomplished if students can read and pronounce words and sentences correctly but have no idea of their meanings. Without certain background information, without actual real-life experiences, without understanding the cultural context in which language is used, students often do not completely comprehend what is said. No lesson should be considered complete until the tutor is satisfied that the words, phrases, and sentences are completely clear to the students. Comprehension is an integral part of language learning; in fact, it is the true foundation of language acquisition.

> *The story is often told of the boy who was asked to read aloud a passage in French. When he finished the teacher asked him to summarize what he'd read. "I can't, sir, I wasn't listening," he commented.*

Language students reading aloud often concentrate so hard on pronouncing the words correctly that they have no idea what they have read.

Because people learn in different ways that are not always predictable or even completely understood by experts on cognition, it's important to know and be able to use different teaching approaches. Condensed descriptions of several techniques will be described here, but you may want to read *TUTOR* (Cheatham, Colvin, Laminack, 1993) for additional information on how to use the following techniques:

- Language Experience
- Sight Words
- Phonics
- Word Patterns
- Process Writing

Language Experience

Language Experience is a recounting in the student's own words of a personal experience, a retelling of a news item, a description, a commentary on a public happening, or anything else of interest to the student. Using Language Experience, you write what the students say, demonstrating the connections between thought and writing, and oral language and written language. Even if your students can't yet read the words, they see how spoken language looks when it becomes written language. The tutor also receives insights into the students' worlds that can guide the tutor in selecting teaching materials.

Invite your students to talk, to tell you something of interest: why they came to America, something about their country's history, their dreams of the future, or issues or problems they are facing (such as looking for a job). Ask questions and pick up ideas from your conversations together. If the students still hesitate to talk, use pictures or articles from magazines or newspapers as a focus for discussion. You might want to write down key words that were used, to prepare them for the next step.

After a discussion, have the students share their thoughts, using the key words as a guide. This can be done on an individual basis or as a group project. Explain that you will write the words they dictate.

Using manuscript writing, write the words spoken or, if you think they're ready, suggest that your students write the words. When beginning-level speakers dictate something incorrectly, it is a good idea to rewrite it in proper English. Say the sentence again and write it correctly. For example, if a student says, *White cat across street ran,* repeat those exact words. Then tell them that in English we say, *The white cat ran across the street.* Let your student decide which sentence she or he wants written in the story. Most ESOL students want to know the correct grammar. Their interest in grammar gives you an oppportunity to model the proper form.

For advanced students you might want to record the exact words. They often know grammatical rules but have not incorporated them into their own spoken language. They sense that something isn't quite right, and when they see their errors in writing they might be more apt to correct themselves. Follow the lead of your students. Suggest that you'll work on more detailed grammar later as the need arises.

If you write on paper, you may want to use carbon paper, too, or if you have access to a photocopy machine, make a photocopy for your student. If you write on a blackboard you may want to copy the words onto paper later.

As you read aloud each student's entire message, pointing to each word, remind the student that these are his or her own words. Then reread the first sentence, again pointing to each word. Ask the student to read that sentence. Continue with the same procedure until he or she reads the story fairly well. If you are working with a small group, you might have the students read aloud together first to gain confidence. Then ask each student to read individually.

Ask the students to pick out five to ten words that they would like to learn separately. Either you or your students should write each word on a small card. Have the students look at each card carefully, reading the word and putting it under its duplicate in the story. Mix the cards up. Then ask the students to read them, referring to the story when necessary.

Have the students reread the story, giving them opportunities to revise or edit. Be sure to give them copies to take home to practice with. If you have one student, make two copies, so you can give the student the original and keep one copy for your files and one for the student's portfolio. With a small group, you might suggest that they copy each story from the blackboard. Making tapes of students reading their own stories is helpful for later evaluation. Self-correcting takes longer in a new language. When you find your students are able to hear "what sounds right," you will see them begin to work more independently.

LANGUAGE EXPERIENCE

1. Invite your students to talk about something of interest to them. Identify key words.

2. After discussion, have the students tell their stories, using the key words as a guide.

3. Write the stories the students dictate or suggest they write them themselves. For beginning non-English-speakers, rewrite the stories in proper English, if needed.

4. Read the entire story, having students read after you. Then reread each sentence, asking the students to repeat after you.

5. Ask the students to select five to ten words that they would like to learn separately. Teach them how to read these words as sight words.

6. Have the students reread the story, giving them opportunities to revise or edit.

Examples of ESOL Language Experience

One student said:

> *America my new country. Portugal my home country. I make new friends. Miss old friends.*

After repeating back what that student said, you might want to correct the English and write:

> *America is my new country. Portugal is my home country. I am making new friends. I miss my old friends.*

The student picked out these words to be put on word cards: *America, country, Portugal, friends.*

A small group of students from three different countries dictated this story:

> *We come America from Vietnam, Poland, China. We want learn English, become good citizens. America like small United Nations.*

The teacher repeated the story with correct grammar and then wrote the story as follows:

> *We came to America from Vietnam, Poland, and China. We want to learn English and become good citizens. America is like a small United Nations.*

The words the students elected to learn first were these: *America, English, citizens, United Nations.*

Margarita, a Spanish-speaking social worker, wanted her tutor to help her write a report to be read to the case conference group she belonged to. She could read English but her writing was limited. Here is what she dictated:

> *I have big problem in community. Is about one mother. She have six children. She not well of the mind. She no feeling well in mind and she go to hospital to get especial attention medicine. We have problem of children now. What do with children?*

Margarita knew that her English was inadequate and was embarrassed to present a report in poor English. She asked if the tutor would please help her put it into "good English." The rewritten story came out like this:

> *I have a big problem in my community. It is about a mother. She has six children. She is not well mentally. She must go to the hospital to get special medical attention. We have the problem of the children. What shall we do with them?*

Margarita read the rewritten story. She was delighted, knowing that she wouldn't be embarrassed at the meeting. While she wasn't able to put her thoughts into standard English yet, learning to do so became a priority for future lessons.

Sight Words and Context Clues

Sight words are those words that students recognize and understand immediately. Such words are learned as whole words. Besides teaching them in experience stories, there are four specific types of words that can be taught as sight words:

SIGHT WORDS

1. Students and tutor select words to be taught as sight words.

2. Ask students each to pick five to ten words, to be learned one at a time.

3. Write that word (in manuscript)—or have students write it—on a word card.

4. Read the word aloud, showing the card, asking students to repeat.

5. Ask students to use the word in a sentence.

6. Go to the next sight word. Repeat the process.

7. Shuffle the word cards and practice rereading them.

8. Put known words in a file. Keep the remainder for further practice.

105

1. survival words: *danger, exit, emergency*

2. service or utility words: *the, of, why*

3. irregularly spelled words: *have, of, laugh*

4. introductory words in word patterns: *run,* then teach *sun, fun, bun*

The tutor and the students together select from the context of the lessons which words are to be learned as sight words. Usually five to ten words per session are all that should be learned. Write in manuscript—or have your students write the words on index cards, one per card. Quartered index cards are also convenient for individual students. Use larger cards for a group. Teach one word at a time.

Say the word as you show the word card. Have the students repeat the word. Ask your students to use the word in a sentence. Have the students look again at the word and repeat the word. Go on to the second word, repeating the process. When you have taught five to eight words, shuffle the word cards and ask the students to read each card.

Generally, if students can read a word out of context on three separate sessions, they know the word and it can be put in a known words file. These can be reviewed periodically to emphasize the many new words the students have learned. These word cards give them something tangible to take home and study.

After or sometimes during a conversation, you and your students can select important new words to write on word cards. Thus, natural conversation can also be a stimulus for building personal word lists that can be taught as sight words.

Sentence Unscrambling

You can give students who read some English, even those at a lower level, a chance to think about language by having them unscramble sentences. On individual cards, write words that the students know. (Make sure that the words together would make a meaningful sentence.) Ask your students to put them in order. They may or may not be in the order you had in mind, but they must make sense. For example:

| *coffee* | *sandwich* | *a* | *I* | *ordered* | *and* |

The sentence could be:

I ordered coffee and a sandwich.

or

I ordered a sandwich and coffee.

You can use lines of a dialogue in place of individual words, asking your students to put each line of the dialogue in a meaningful order. Or you can jumble the sentences of any given paragraph, suggesting that the students put the sentences together so that they make sense. You can also cut apart a comic strip and have the students put the frames in the proper order.

Sentence Unscrambling

Tutor gives word cards or sentence cards in random order, asking the students to put them in proper sequence.

the   vegetables   bought   store   father   at   the

The father bought vegetables at the store.

Phonics: Letter-Sound Relationships

Effective reading necessitates that students make accurate connections between sounds and letters or groups of letters. Many languages are phonetically regular (i.e., letters or groups of letters always represent the same sounds). While English is not phonetically regular, particularly the vowel sounds, most consonants represent a constant sound. Those students who can read and write in a language with Roman letters will probably know that the sounds these same consonants represent in their language do not sound too different from English. For those students who cannot read or write in their own language, or for those whose written language does not use Roman letters, understanding phonics will probably be more difficult.

Teaching Consonants

The sounds of the consonants in English are more constant than the sounds of the vowels. To help your students with their consonants, work with them to create a letter-sound dictionary. Use one sheet of paper, an index card, or one page of an address book for each letter. You might start with *m, f,* and *s.* Because the sounds of these letters are sustained, they're usually easier to learn. Indicate the sounds of letters by writing them with slash marks on either side: */m/, /f/, /s/.* Consonant digraphs, in which two letters together represent one sound *(ch, sh, th, wh,* or *qu)*, are taught the same way as consonants are taught.

Alternatively, you may want to start with a consonant in your student's name or in his or her country. It is not necessary to learn the sounds in alphabetical order. Start with letters that might be most useful to the student. They can be put in alphabetical order later. Detailed discussion and instructions are included in *TUTOR* and should be reviewed, but here is the abbreviated version.

1. Identify the letter by saying its name and writing it in manuscript.

    This is the letter m. *What is the name of this letter?* (m)

2. Ask the student to listen to the beginning sound.

    Listen for the sound of m *at the beginning of these words and repeat the words* motor (motor), mother (mother), milk (milk).

3. Ask the student to pick a key word and write the key word under the letter.

    *Which of these words—*motor, mother, milk—*do you want to help you remember the sound of* m? (motor)

4. Ask the student to produce the beginning sound.

    Think of the beginning sound in motor *and say the first sound.* (/m/) /m/ *is the first sound of the letter* m.

5. See if the student recognizes the sound in other words.

    Here are other words. Listen. Do they start with the /m/ sound? Country. (No) *Miles.* (Yes) *Telephone.* (No) *Moon.* (Yes) *Family.* (No)

6. Put the sound at the end of words.

    *I'll move the /m/ sound to the end of words. Listen to the last sound and repeat the words—*rim (rim), them (them), thumb (thumb). (Note to the tutor: It doesn't matter that the spelling isn't regular, if the last sound is /m/).

7. Have the student produce the ending sound.

    What is the last sound in these words? (/m/)

8. Review the name of each letter, its key word, and its sound.

    What is the name of this letter? (m) *What is your key word?* (motor) *What is the sound at the beginning of the word?* (/m/)

9. Have the student write the letter.

    Please write an m. (The student writes an m.)

10. Explain and write the capital letter.

    This is a capital M, the same name, the same sound. Write a capital M. (The student writes a capital M.)

Consonant digraphs, in which two letters together represent one sound *(ch, sh, th, wh,* or *qu)*, are taught in the same way as consonants are taught.

Word Patterns (Teaching Vowels in Pattern)

Vowels in English have many sounds. Note the different sounds of the letter *a* in the following words:

can

came

call

car

English may not always be phonetically regular, but it is generally a patterned language: *an, ame, all,* and *ar* are constant patterns. You can teach vowels through their various patterns—*can, ran, pan; came, game, same; call, fall, ball; car, tar, bar.*

Learning words by seeing word patterns helps students to notice the relationships between clusters of letters and the sounds they represent. Parts of words that sound alike are often spelled alike.

Choose a patterned word from the words your students already know. Use a simple consonant-vowel-consonant (C-V-C) word first. This word will provide a clue that will help them figure out the other words in that pattern. Be sure the students understand the meaning of the words you use, know about rhyming, and are familiar with some of the consonant sounds, which will help them to master the word pattern technique. Teaching words in pattern may seem simple, but it is well worth practicing because of its value.

It is helpful to write the words as they are spoken, listing them in a column so that similar letters in the pattern can be seen as well as heard. Here are the basic steps for teaching words in pattern:

1. Write the first word in the pattern: *man*
   followed by the second patterned word: *pan*

2. Explain as follows:
   If m-a-n *is man, what is* p-a-n?

3. If the student responds correctly,   *ran*
   add more words in pattern.   *can*

   Ask the student to read them.

   If the student gives no response or responds incorrectly, think about possible learning blocks:

   • He or she may not know the sound of the consonant *(p,r,c).*

   • He or she may not know the sound of the vowel or vowel cluster. *(an)*

- Ask the student to identify the letters that are the same in all the words.

4. Make word cards for the words in pattern.

English has many unusual spellings, but once a pattern is learned, your students will find they can read many more words. (See word lists in appendix of *TUTOR*.)

sight	*oil*
might	*soil*
light	*toil*
blight	*boil*

Process Writing

Writing is one of the four skills—listening, speaking, reading, writing—needed to learn a new language. Writing is one form of giving information, and writing in English is a highly useful communication skill in today's world. While help may be available, the independence of students is enhanced if they can fill out their own job applications, write their own letters to loved ones, write their own reports, take notes during a lecture, write their own checks and financial reports—the list is endless. Writing will also help students see what they have learned and help them to remember it.

Language Experience can be *written* by students as well as dictated. The same life experiences, stories, and interests can be expressed in writing just as they were expressed orally. If your students can write the Roman letters, they can start writing just as soon as they have heard and understood, spoken, and read even a few words. Here we will focus on writing a simple or complex report or story.

1. A **trigger event** starts a discussion. This could be a picture, a special interest in reminiscing about your students' homeland, or a discussion of a hobby or profession (e.g., comparing a nurse's training in the Ukraine with that of the United States). Time spent in discussion of trigger events will stimulate good ideas for writing.

2. **Prewriting** activities include discussion of whatever topic was selected. They could involve simply describing a picture or retelling a news event, or they could respond to a real need such as writing a letter to their children's teacher. The tutor can lead the discussion, asking questions and encouraging the students to participate. The students must then decide which type of writing task they want to do. They may want to write a letter, a report, or a story.

3. **Brainstorm** together about the trigger event, jot down **key words.** These can become a simple outline of what the students want to

write. From these key words, the students begin to **write**. This can be an individual project or a group project. If students write individually, assure them that you are not looking for correct spelling, proper grammar, or correct punctuation. At this time, you want them to get their ideas down on paper. If the students write in groups, have them select one person to write on the board or flip chart what the others dictate. Again, spelling, grammar, and punctuation are not a concern at this time.

4. Next have the students **read aloud** what was written. Accept their words and their pronunciations. Only comment on grammar or pronunciation if they ask for help. Let them know that you understand what they have written. Then **discuss** the content of what students have written, asking for clarification of ideas where necessary.

5. Based on this discussion, the students will often suggest changes to their writing. They are **revising** and **rewriting** their own work—a most important step. They can continue to revise and rewrite until their work is the way they want it. As a final step, encourage your students to type their work on a computer or typewriter if they have access to one. Make photocopies to give to the students.

PROCESS WRITING

1. Select trigger event
2. Prewrite
   a. Discuss
   b. Decide on the writing task
   c. Brainstorm—write key words
3. Write
4. Read, respond, and discuss
5. Revise and rewrite

Journals and Letter Writing

Many ESOL students are interested in and willing to try writing their own experiences and thoughts if they are assured that their work will be kept confidential. Encourage them to write even a sentence or two each day in a journal. They can review their writing later if they want to, or use it as a nonthreatening way to practice putting their thoughts down on paper.

Letters to and from people who are important to the students can be meaningful. Students may want to write letters to their families and friends in their native languages, or they may want to try writing in English—letters to their children's teachers, letters of complaint for defective merchandise, letters to accompany job applications, or letters to you. You should respond as you do to any other letter, modeling through your response the correct ways to write things in English. Never correct journal entries. If something is incomprehensible, just ask for clarification, when you write back.

Grammar and Sentence Structure

Some ESOL students feel that grammar and sentence structure are basic to learning English. It is often difficult to assure them that they will learn correct English grammar and sentence structure not by rules but by listening to fluent speakers like you. Most of us do not stop and think about the correct way to say something—whether the noun comes first, or whether we are talking in the present or present progressive tense. We just know when it sounds right. We want to help our students get a feel for the language, too.

Language is best learned in real-life contexts, whether it is in general conversation, reading, or writing. Rules of grammar should probably be delayed until after students have used English in specific real-life situations. After students can understand, speak, and have general conversations, you can explain pertinent grammar rules. This can happen even after students understand and can only say simple sentences like *I go to the supermarket*. If they want rules, you can explain, for example, that in English the subject goes before the verb. We never say:

To the supermarket go I.   or   *I to the supermarket go.*

Many textbooks have suggestions for practicing correct sentence structure. Use them creatively to supplement your lessons.

Some students want help in more advanced grammar usage. For example, you might want to teach the present progressive tense. You could do this by bringing objects to help your students understand (pennies to count, cookies to eat, paper clips to put in a box). Tell the students to count the pennies, eat the cookies, or put the paper clips in the box. Then ask the students what they are doing. As they are counting the pennies, they may say, *I count pennies*. You may want to model the correct answer first, or you may want to let them try for themselves. They may get the correct answers because they have heard similar English sentences. You may get these answers:

We count pennies.

We eat cookies.

We put paper clips in the box.

You can model the correct replies, having them repeat:

We are (or we're) counting pennies.

We are (or we're) eating cookies.

We are (or we're) putting paper clips in the box.

If you are working on the past progressive verb tense, have the students do the same activities listed above (count pennies, eat cookies, put paper clips in a box). Ring a bell, clap your hands, or knock on the table to stop the activity. Ask your students what they were doing when you gave the signal to stop.

The correct responses would be:

We were counting pennies.

We were eating cookies.

We were putting paper clips in the box.

It is not important that they, or you, can name the verb tense. It is important that they just know how to use tenses when talking about an action that they are or were doing.

For the present, past, and future tenses, you could use a newspaper ad showing groceries and their prices. Say that you are going to plan a shopping list. Ask your students to indicate what to buy by stating it in a sentence:

Today we are buying (or we're buying) tomatoes. The price is $. . ..

Yesterday we bought bread. The price was $. . ..

Tomorrow we will buy (or we'll buy or we're going to buy) lettuce. The price will be $. . ..

You can vary the items by using different ads—such as those for clothing, hardware, or household items—depending on students' interests.

Teacher-made exercises can be used for practicing various parts of speech or grammar. Use any material of interest to your students. Copy any article of interest (a newspaper article about sports, a travel story of a faraway place, a descriptive article on food, etc.). White out whatever part of speech you're working on (e.g., all prepositions). Read aloud the entire article to your students. Then read the article again, omitting the prepositions, having the students supply them. If it's a beginning group, have a list of the prepositions available. If it's an advanced group, let them supply the prepositions. Finally, give the students copies of the articles with the prepositions missing, having each of them fill in the correct words. You can create this exercise with missing nouns, verbs, adjectives, or other grammatical forms.

For students who want to learn the details of English grammar, many textbooks and workbooks are available. Look these over with your students as you choose books that fit individual needs. Use them creatively.

Reading to Expand Vocabulary

Most literate Americans who have expanded their vocabularies have done so by reading, reading, and reading some more. Encourage your students to read everything around them. You can use print materials—labels, TV ads, billboards—as the basis for further discussion to help stimulate vocabulary development and fluency of expression.

While we encourage our students to listen and speak before reading new material, there comes a time when they should begin independent reading.

The timing varies from student to student, but when students can read fairly well, perhaps at the *ESLOA* Level III or IV, you might encourage them to read material that is slightly above their level. Suggest that they read fast, skimming each page. When they ask for help with unknown words, have them guess the meanings, using context clues. All proficient readers do this—they learn new words just by reading; they don't look up the meaning of each word they read. ESOL students can be taught to figure out the meanings of new vocabulary words in their reading as well.

Reading Aloud

Reading poetry aloud or reading excerpts from plays can give pronunciation practice. Real-life stress, rhythm, and intonation patterns can be practiced without specific drills. You can have the students read with you or "shadow" your reading, following your natural speech patterns. This exercise gives practice in reading aloud articles or stories of interest to the students as they follow your own speech rhythms and intonation. Use a tape recorder if possible so that students can read aloud and then listen to their own pronunciation, rhythm, and intonation.

More Comprehension Checks

Continue to check comprehension as your students read, as well as when they listen and speak. You can always ask questions. One suggestion is to turn subtitles in a text or story into questions. If the story is about food and the subtitle is "Pancakes", ask what pancakes are. There are other ways to check comprehension as well.

If students can put the events in a story or text in the right order, they have probably comprehended what they have read or heard. You might read or tell a story to your students. Have available pictures depicting the story, but not in sequence. Together discuss the story and have your students put the pictures in the right order. This can also be done with comic strips. Cut the comic strip apart, mix the frames up, and have your students put them in sequence, using the pictures as well as the words as clues.

You can do this with reading as well. Before the lesson, cut apart a story with separate paragraphs (or sentences) pasted on separate cards. Mix the cards up so they are not in sequence. After you have read the story to your students, or after they have read it, have the students read the paragraphs (or sentences) again and put them in the right order.

SUMMARY

Use and adapt the techniques and exercises described in this chapter to help your students pursue their needs and interests and attain their goals. Include all four skills—listening/understanding, speaking, reading, writing—but accommodate to each student's needs and learning style. After your students can understand and speak English competently, encourage them to read new material for pleasure or for knowledge, and encourage them to write, to put their ideas and concerns on paper. As a general rule, all of the language communication skills should be integrated into your work, regardless of the levels of your students, even if you are only stressing one or two of the skills in a particular lesson.

The Communicative Approach, as suggested in this book,

- stresses comprehension
- uses all four language skills—listening, speaking, reading, writing
- encourages the use of authentic, real-life material and vocabulary
- is learner centered and learner directed
- is collaborative, in that the students are involved in all parts of the lessons

Mix and match the suggested techniques, exercises, and activities, adapting them to the materials and vocabulary needed by the students.

Literacy Volunteers of America, Inc.

RESOURCES AND MORE ACTIVITIES

CHAPTER

VIII

- ◆ **RESOURCES**
- ◆ **MORE ACTIVITIES**
- ◆ **SUMMARY**

CHAPTER VIII
RESOURCES AND MORE ACTIVITIES

There are many resources and activities to help your students become proficient in English. Your library and affiliate resource files will have suggestions, but you need to be creative and to work closely with your students to identify which specific skills and topics of interest to focus on.

RESOURCES

Survival Kit

In order to meet many basic needs in a society whose dominant language is different than one's own, it is desirable to understand and speak, read, and write specific words and phrases in that language. Such mastery is what we refer to as "survival skills." Teaching these survival skills should be a part of early lessons with any students who haven't yet developed them. It is recommended that early in your teaching you check out individual students' abilities to handle these skills so that you know which skills need further development and practice. Many examples of survival skill activities can be found in *The Competency-Based-Mainstream English Language Training (MELT)* suggestion guide in the appendix.

As you prepare for your first lesson, get the necessary items for a Survival Kit to keep in a folder or bag for easy reference. It will not only help you in your first lesson but will also provide lesson topics relevant to your students' needs for portions of future lessons. Here are some suggested items. Add others as you see the need.

- students' names, addresses, and telephone numbers
- letter names
- neighborhood, United States, and world maps
- number cards
- price tags
- money—coins and "play" bills
- students' clothing sizes
- cardboard clock
- calendar
- sample restaurant menu
- bus/train schedule
- bilingual dictionary
- mirror for use in teaching pronunciation

Literacy Volunteers of America, Inc.

Student's Names, Addresses, and Telephone Numbers

Most ESOL students can repeat their names and addresses in English. Stress the importance of keeping a written copy of this information with them. Often native English-speakers cannot understand non-native English-speakers because of strong accents and hence cannot give proper directions when asked. By modeling the correct pronunciation of students' addresses and telephone numbers, you help them avoid an embarrassing or frightening experience. Putting that information on a tape recorder will give your students opportunities to practice at home.

Letter Names

When someone cannot understand a word as spoken, the listener often asks the speaker to spell it. Whether students' native languages use the Roman alphabet or not, they need to learn the names of the letters in English.

You can use regular or quartered 3" x 5" cards, writing both the lower-and uppercase letter of the alphabet on each card. To teach letter names, pronounce the name of each letter, point to the letter, and have your students repeat it. You might start with the names of the letters in your students' names, writing the letters in manuscript as you repeat the letter names.

L-u-p-e R-i-v-e-r-a

You may find certain letters are confusing to your students because they sound or look somewhat alike:

a and *e*

i and *y*

c, z, and *s*

b, p, v, and *f*

g and *j*

Have your students repeat the names of letters until they can

- say the name of each letter as you point at random
- point to the correct letter as you say the letter name

Visual Aids

Tools for teaching conversational English are endless. Using visual materials helps promote understanding, giving your students opportunities to associate words with actual objects or pictures. Picture dictionaries are available, but you may want to create your own library of pictures of objects or activities according to student interest. Although visual aids are particularly important with beginning-level students, they can be used creatively with all students to stimulate vocabulary development, free conversation, and student writing.

Real Objects

The most practical visual aids for building conversation and expanding vocabulary are real objects such as table, chair, window, pencil, book, clothing (yours and your students'), or whatever is available. After the students can say the words and identify the objects when you or other students say them, you might want to label them or have your students label them so they can practice reading them. Use all the techniques you have learned, including asking questions.

How many windows are there?

What color is my sweater?

Suggest that your students bring in objects or pictures of objects they want to identify in English. Items which are common to your students' lives can stimulate conversation—a watch, articles of clothing, pots and pans, a portable radio.

A handbag suggests words like *handle, leather,* and *mirror.*

A sewing kit suggests *needle, thread,* and *scissors.*

A box of cereal suggests words like *box, cardboard,* and *top.*

A dish suggests *round, glass,* and *bottom.*

There are endless ways to encourage conversation. Gradually encourage the students to ask questions. This not only provides speaking practice, but might even satisfy your students' curiosity about why Americans use or do certain things. If you are teaching a lesson on how to open a bank account, bring deposit and withdrawal slips and, if possible, an actual savings account passbook. The more the senses are employed, the more likely the learning will stick. An actual orange has weight, fragrance, and color, and its name will be fixed in the students' minds through their senses of touch, sight, and smell. Use real objects whenever possible; if you can't get real objects, use pictures.

Pictures and Picture File

It is sometimes impractical to bring real-life situations into your teaching sessions, but you can always bring in pictures. For introducing new words, even in a simple substitution drill, pictures can reveal a meaning immediately and help make it memorable.

Pictures from catalogs, magazines, newspapers, calendars, advertisements, maps, photographs, or postcards can be useful for teaching English. It is wise to collect these illustrations before their need arises. A doctor's office, a beauty salon, or a barber shop may be good places to pick up free issues of magazines with useful pictures.

File your pictures by topic for ready reference. Mounting pictures on heavy paper or cardboard keeps them from getting ruined. Pictures generally fall into two categories:

- those illustrating a single object or action
- those depicting an entire situation

As you start to collect pictures, you might find the following suggestions helpful:

- Cut out everything you think you might use. It is often difficult to locate pictures you need for a specific lesson when you want them.

- Select pictures that illustrate a specific object, place, individual, scene, or action.

- Select pictures that depict an entire situation that could be used as a topic for conversation (e.g., a family picnic).

- Collect pictures that illustrate contrasts (e.g. big/small, fat/thin, happy/sad, wide/narrow) or which represent concepts that are difficult to describe (e.g., above, under, between, up, down, numbers, colors).

- Look for pictures that depict emotions: love, hate, jealousy, arrogance, kindness.

- Although many pictures in your file will reflect American culture, include some pictures of other cultures. Ask your students to share pictures of their native cultures as well.

- Avoid using pictures with extraneous printing on them that may be confusing.

- Set up a simple set of categories:

  ▶ animals (cats, dogs, other animals)

  ▶ body (arm, leg, head, hair)

  ▶ clothing (men's, women's, children's)

  ▶ colors, shapes, sizes (red/blue, round/square, big/small)

  ▶ family (mother, father, children, grandparents)

  ▶ food (vegetables, meals)

  ▶ household (kitchen appliances, bedroom, bath)

  ▶ occupations/jobs (clerk, carpenter, team leader)

  ▶ problems (pictures which portray problems students may face—hospital scenes, inadequate housing, etc.)

  ▶ recreation/sports (soccer, baseball, swimming)

  ▶ seasons (spring, summer, fall/autumn, winter)

▶ transportation (boat, bus, car, plane, train)

Add any other categories you find might be helpful on the back of the pictures, identify them and write questions or suggestions for using them.

These picture files can be shared with your affiliate or group.

Clocks

Americans are usually very time conscious. Many activities in this country are governed by the clock. If you are working with your student on telling time, you may want to use a digital clock. If you are using a traditional clock, you can bring a clock, adjusting the hands, or you can make one out of cardboard or a paper plate.

In America, if a bus is scheduled to leave at 10:42 a.m., it doesn't mean "about" that time. If you have a dental appointment at 9:30 a.m., you had better be there a few minutes early. Because this idea of time and punctuality is not universal, you should discuss the ideas that many Americans have about time. Encourage your students to write their appointments in a date book.

To teach time using a clock, start with the hours: 1:00 is *one o'clock*, 2:00 is *two o'clock*, etc. Then 1:30 is *one-thirty*, 2:30 is *two-thirty*. Follow this by 1:15 is *one-fifteen*, or *fifteen after one*, or *quarter past one*. Be consistent by using only one form at the beginning, giving alternates later. Take your cue from your students if they speak some English. For example, if they say *quarter to two*, reinforce that before giving alternates.

Realize, too, that as much as Americans tend to go rigidly "by the clock," there are some situations that require being early.

- An air flight time of 1:30 means you should arrive at the airport at least one hour early for boarding (for international flights, two hours early) because the plane actually leaves the ground at 1:30.

- A clinic appointment at 2:30 p.m. means you should arrive a few minutes early.

- A 9-to-5 job means exactly that: arrive before nine to be ready to start at 9:00 and work until 5:00, except for lunch and breaks.

- An invitation to a reception or a party "from 6 to 8" means you arrive sometime after 6:00 and leave before or at 8:00. Guests are not expected to arrive before the stated time.

Calendars

Students should also learn how to use a calendar if they do not already know how. In fact, a calendar is a useful device for teaching and practicing English. Pronounce the months of the year and the days of the week as you point to them on the calendar. You might want to provide your students with calendars, indicating the days of your lessons as well as other important information.

Your students may or may not be able to say the names of the months or the days of the week. Model them and have the students repeat. But also be sure your students hear and understand them. You could say *Tuesday*, and ask the students to point on the calendar to the appropriate column.

One student couldn't understand why his fellow workers laughed when he said he'd be back on *thirsty*. He said, with a question in his eyes, *Sunday, Monday, Tuesday, Wednesday, Thirsty?* Gently the tutor explained the difference between *thirsty* and *Thursday*. Incorrect pronunciation can completely change the meaning of a word.

Telephones

The telephone is considered a necessity by most people in America. However, it is much more difficult to converse on a telephone than to talk directly to a person since you cannot see the speaker's face, eyes, or gestures.

If you have visited another country and speak little of the language of that country, you know what a frustrating experience talking on the telephone can be. How do you dial? What do you say to the operator?

Many practical lessons can be planned around the use of the telephone. It provides an excellent introduction to dialogue, because a telephone conversation is just that—a dialogue between two people. You can use a toy telephone that has a a touch-tone key pad or a dial, or you may want to draw a set of numbers resembling a touch-tone key pad or make a cardboard phone dial. You and your student, or two students back-to-back, can simulate a real telephone conversation. Then, for reinforcement, students can actually call you and each other from their homes.

Numbers and Money

Numbers should be among the first items taught. They are important in everyday life. Think how often they are needed: telephone numbers, house numbers, prices, weights, and sizes.

Numbers must be exact. Whereas mispronunciation of some words or poor grammar can be tolerated, a mispronounced number cannot. When discussing prices, even knowing where to put the word dollars is important. *Two hundred fifty dollars* is very different from *two dollars and fifty cents.*

Will Durant, in *Our Oriental Heritage* (1954), writes that "Counting was probably one of the earliest forms of speech and in many tribes it still presents a relieving simplicity. The Tasmanians counted up to two: 'Parmery, calabawa, cardia', i.e., one, two, plenty; the Guaranis of Brazil adventured further and said: 'One, two, three, four, innumerable.' . . . Counting was by the fingers, hence the decimal system. When, apparently after some time, the idea of twelve was reached, the number became a favorite because it was pleasantly divisible by five of the first six digits; and that duodecimal system was born which obstinately survives in English measurement today; twelve units in a dozen, twelve dozen in a gross, twelve inches in a foot. Thirteen, on the other hand, refused to be divided, and became disreputable and unlucky forever."

How would you say these numbers?

1776: You would probably say *seventeen seventy-six* because you assume it's a date. But it could be *one, seven, seven, six* or *seventeen hundred and seventy-six* or *one thousand seven hundred and seventy-six.*

437-8381: *Four, three, seven, eight, three, eight, one* because you assume it's a telephone number. But it could be *four hundred thirty-seven dash eight thousand three hundred eighty-one.*

$3.50: *Three dollars and fifty cents* or *three fifty* or *three-and-a-half dollars.* All mean the same thing to most Americans.

1249: *Twelve forty-nine,* for example, for an address, or *one thousand two hundred forty-nine.*

6.2: *Six point two* or *six and two-tenths.*

1/10: *One-tenth.*

Imagine how confusing it must be to students to learn that we say the same number in many ways. Your students must not only be able to say the numbers, knowing which numbers they mean (*seventy-nine* is 79 and *ninety-seven* is 97), but also recognize them when they hear them. If *seventeen nine* (179) is heard when you say *seventy-nine* (79), there will probably be many problems. Students may have difficulty distinguishing among *nine, nineteen, ninety,* and *ninth.*

To help them, give your students a list of the first ten numbers, pointing to each number as you say it, and ask them to repeat it several times. Review at the end of ten numbers. When you feel your students know the names of these numbers, point to them at random, asking for the names of the numbers. This is a bit more difficult, and you may find your students counting silently *(one, two, three, four, five, six)* to get to *seven*. Then say a number and have the students point to it. Usually it is more difficult to hear and point to a number than to see the number and say its name.

Reverse the roles. Have a student say a number, and you or another student point to it. Sometimes one number will be spoken when another is intended. Perhaps a student will say *eighteen* (18) and mean *eighty* (80). This will make quite a difference if it refers to a price or an address.

Continue introducing numbers 11 through 19. Then teach 20, 30, 40, 50, etc.

Teach numbers that are said individually (telephone numbers and some addresses) before moving on to numbers said in chunks. Teach the different ways of saying prices. $2.98 is *two dollars and ninety-eight cents,* or *two ninety-eight* for short. Reverse the process and have the students take turns giving the prices. Write down the figures that they dictate. Are they the same as what they intended?

Continue by asking questions or giving directions where the students must think in numerical terms:

> *How many windows are there in the room?*
>
> *How many days are in a year?*
>
> *Turn to page 362.*

If the students can add, divide, and multiply in their own languages, provide simple mathematical problems in English. This will help to develop their fluency and build their skills.

Even more advanced students need a lot of repetition hearing and saying numbers. Vary the ways you give this practice. You can dictate numbers, using statistics, prices, times, and telephone numbers, giving the students opportunities to hear big and complex numbers as well as simple or more familiar ones. Repeat your dictation at least once, giving the students an opportunity to hear the numbers again and check their own papers to be sure they've written what they heard. If you have a small group, ask each student to prepare a list of numbers and dictate them to another student or to the group. Thus, students must pronounce the numbers so that others can understand them. If you are teaching only one student, tape another person's voice for your student to hear. Give that student an opportunity to dictate numbers to you.

Most countries use the metric system. Some organizations in the United States are gradually changing over to this system. Until the metric system is universal, your students must know our present system of measurements: an inch, a foot, a yard, clothing sizes. You can help your students with their personal shopping by preparing a written list of each one's sizes after converting them to the American system. For example:

suit: size 36 regular

shirt: 15/32

underwear: 34-36 medium

socks: size 9-12

shoes: size 10B

dress: size 14

It is important for students to know their height in feet and inches and weight in pounds when filling in medical and insurance forms. You could help them take their own measurements and weigh themselves by bringing a tape measure and small scale to a lesson. It might be helpful for them to know that some American women might tell you how tall they are but will seldom divulge their weight or their age. This is so because youth and slimness are glamorized in America.

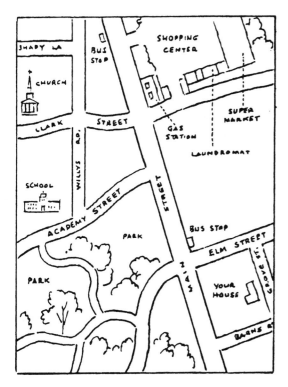

Maps, Directions

Some non-English-speakers are hesitant to venture from their homes. The fear of getting lost because they cannot communicate is real, so it seems safer to stay indoors or nearby. You can help your students feel more comfortable about venturing out alone by working with them to make a simple neighborhood map.

First discuss how the students get from their homes to the tutoring place, noting landmarks and streets. You may have to supply the street names. Note the major points of interest or landmarks with pictures or stick figures and print the names of major streets on a sketch of the area to be mapped.

Then you might take a walk with your students, following the map, making corrections or additions as appropriate. The freedom and confidence a simple individualized neighborhood map provides will broaden your students' day-to-day living.

Use that same map as a visual aid, starting with listening comprehension techniques. You might say:

> *Point to the school.*
>
> *Point to the supermarket.*

Then ask for simple directions in English:

> *Where is the church?*
>
> *Where is the library?*

Continue with practical responses in English:

> *It's straight ahead.*
>
> *Go one block and turn right and then go two blocks and turn left.*

Maps can also be made for taking public transportation. Venturing alone on a bus can be a big undertaking. Make a simple map, showing the number of blocks and where the bus turns. If it is appropriate, go with your students for the first time, pointing out landmarks.

If your students are unable to ask the bus driver for help, write a note to be carried along or teach these instructions:

> *Please tell me when the bus gets to Main and Elm Streets.*

Using a world map, students can indicate where their countries are in relation to the United States. An enlarged map of their countries gives them opportunities to show you more specifically where they used to live. They may even want to talk about their friends and their families back home.

My Family Tree

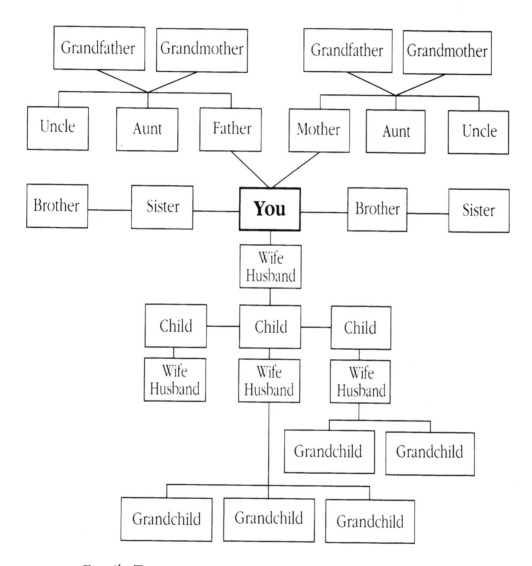

Family Tree

Respect for ancestors and elders is important in many cultures. Doing research together to find out about your students' forebears can be a rewarding project.

Your own family tree could be a model for your students' family trees, as you show and tell about your own parents, grandparents, and children.

Have each student write his or her name in the center box, gradually adding names of other members of their families. The students are the experts on their families; you are not. Just say, *Tell me about your family,* and let them talk in English about their families and their homelands. Remember that their families may consist of more, fewer, or different individuals than yours. They may also have lost family members in a war or left some behind, so be sensitive to their reservations and emotions.

Simple Drawings

You may want to draw a picture to help teach a word or an action or a concept that can't wait for a more formal illustration. You can make your own stick figures to illustrate a word or action; you need not be an artist to do this. Note the simple steps you can use:

head

head and trunk

(legs added) head, trunk, and legs

(arms added) head, trunk, legs, and arms

(male figure) stick figure with pants

(female figure) stick figure with skirt

Now let's try to illustrate a sentence.

The man is sitting and reading.

or

A man is sitting in a chair reading.

The woman picked the flower from the garden.

or

A girl is smelling a flower.

Note that the same picture can be used with either the present or the past tense, depending on the verb, as in this picture. It's fun; you will all laugh; you will have communicated.

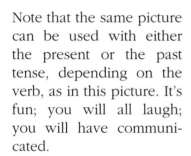

Bilingual Dictionary

A bilingual dictionary, with words from both English and the student's or students' languages, can be a big help. Use real objects or pictures, when possible, to communicate word meanings, encouraging the students to link English words directly with images, and avoiding translations. Naturally, there are times when abstract words such as *beauty, challenge,* or *understanding* are difficult to explain by demonstration or pictures, in which case a dictionary may come in handy.

If your students can read in their native language, look the difficult word up in the bilingual dictionary, having the students read that word in their own language. Many students want to make their own bilingual dictionaries, writing new words in both English and their native language. An easy way to do this is to get an address book already labeled from A to Z. Students can easily add new words. A plain sheet of paper for each letter in the alphabet works well, too. If your students cannot read in their native languages, you should try to pronounce the word in the student's language using the phonetic symbols in the bilingual dictionary.

Bilingual dictionaries can be very helpful, but they should be used sparingly and carefully. Be sure you have the right part of speech, and if more than one definition is given, read the whole dictionary entry to see what other English meanings are given.

This point is illustrated in the following story:

> *I was writing to my Spanish-speaking friend in Mexico. I wanted to begin the letter with the greeting which is traditional in American culture:* Dear Lupe. *I looked up* dear *in the Spanish-English dictionary, where I found the Spanish words* caro, cara. *Confidently I wrote:* Cara Lupe.
>
> *It wasn't until months later that I learned that* cara *means* costly *or* expensive, *and thus* dear. *The next time I wrote to my Spanish friend I used the correct word:* querida.

Even if you happen to know your student's language, use English during the lesson time. Occasionally it can be helpful to explain something in the student's language when you have difficulty getting the meaning across in other ways. Use a bilingual dictionary only to translate the words you are having real trouble explaining.

Textbooks

Good ESOL textbooks can provide a logical, incrementally difficult sequence for teaching vocabulary, grammar and usage, pronunciation, and comprehension. Since they progress gradually, they can be used both with students who can read and write some English as well as with those who can't read or write at all. Some books are now available that have only pictures, no words. These are invaluable as basic tools for teaching conversational English, as they stimulate drill substitution and vocabulary and phrase building with beginning-level students and more extensive dialogues with advanced students.

Use textbooks as guides, but don't depend on them totally. Be creative in how you use them, keeping in mind that they can help give continuity to your lessons. Look over several textbooks (see the appendix for guidelines on selecting textbooks). You may feel more comfortable with one particular text, finding it more appropriate for your students. If practical, ask your students to help select the text(s). After you have chosen a textbook, use it as a guide for follow-up or to reinforce any part of your lesson. Textbooks necessarily have printed words. But if you read the foreword or teacher's guide, you'll discover that many authors suggest that the lessons be introduced by listening/speaking, not by reading.

Some textbooks have simple placement tests which you may wish to use. Start your lessons at the point where your students falter or show little understanding. Students may have a fairly good vocabulary and may understand singular and plural, negatives and questions, and present tense. However, they may have problems with the past tense. Review quickly the earlier lessons in that text and concentrate on the lessons where they need help. Don't be misled into thinking your students understand because they nod their heads. A nod is often a polite way to show appreciation for what you are doing and may cover the anxiety associated with not comprehending.

Some of the following points are stressed in good ESOL textbooks and are listed here as a reminder to take a comprehensive approach with any resource or material.

- Give a simple explanation of the purpose of the lesson, perhaps showing some of the pictures in the book.

- Read aloud the sentences or paragraphs, suggesting that the students not look at the book.

- Ask your students to tell in their own words what you read. They can ask questions, and you can ask questions to check comprehension.

- If there are questions or exercises to be done at the end of the text book lesson, read those questions aloud to the students, asking them to respond verbally. You might want to read the questions aloud before reading the text, giving them an idea of what to look for.

- Give the students copies of the sentences or paragraphs you read aloud. Have the students read the same words, first silently, then aloud. This way you can check their pronunciation.

- Have the students read silently the questions or exercises at the end of the lesson, asking them to respond orally as well as in writing.

- Go over the written exercises to correct grammar, spelling, or punctuation.

Don't overlook children's books. Many of them have wonderful illustrations which stimulate conversation. Also, the children's section of the library contains books that concentrate on specific competencies, such as grammar. Some simply written books are all in the past tense; others are in the present or future tense. Another invaluable source are books for adult basic education students; they're actually written for adults. Many are written by students themselves.

Be selective as you use textbooks to fit into your own individualized lesson plans.

MORE ACTIVITIES

Colored Paper Exercises (adapted from Gattegno [1963]).

Using colored strips of paper as props is an excellent and entertaining exercise, especially for students who understand or speak very limited or no English. You will be teaching simple sentences, and you can add new vocabulary as quickly or as slowly as students respond.

Have on hand the following materials:

Slips of colored paper—blue, red, black, yellow, etc., sizes 1"x 6", 1"x 5", 1"x 3" for each color

The vocabulary used will be controlled and limited to the following words during this part of the lesson:

Lesson 1 *a, paper, blue, red, pick, up, put, on, the, table*

Lesson 2 *give, me, point, to, black, yellow, take*

Lesson 3 *touch, it, him, her, one, two, three*

Lesson 4 *white, green, down*

Lesson 5 *on, under, between, (more colors)*

Lesson 6 *big, bigger, biggest, small, smaller, smallest*

Lesson 7 *next, here, there*

Lesson 8 *right, left, hand, quickly, slowly*

Lesson 9 *other useful words*

For the first lesson, use three blue and three red pieces of paper of varied sizes. The new vocabulary will include only basic words that go along with your actions. Your students do not see these words written but hear you say them when you demonstrate with the pieces of paper. At first your students may try to repeat what you say. Discourage this by gesturing that the students should listen only.

Pick up any slip of paper, either color, any size, and say, *A paper,* at a normal speed. Repeat this with each piece of paper. Repetition gives students confidence that they understood you. Then pick up a blue piece of paper, any size, and say, *A blue paper,* repeating for each blue piece of paper. Repeat this action with the red papers. Next pick up a blue paper and say, *Pick up a blue paper.* Repeat this with all the blue and red papers. Next put each paper on the table as you say, *Put a blue (red) paper on the table.*

When you feel your students have understood your demonstration, push the six pieces of paper to one student and tell the student, *Pick up a red paper.* If your student hesitates and doesn't understand, you can help by motioning him to pick up the red paper. After the student has picked up all the papers say, *Put a red (blue) paper on the table.* Give help as needed. This exercise should be repeated for each student.

Next, gesture for your students to *repeat,* and go through the entire exercise again, starting with a *paper,* demonstrating while you speak and your students repeat.

Finally, suggest that the students give the commands, asking you or other students to demonstrate with appropriate papers. This demonstrates that they understand and can give the commands.

Now it is time for you to write all the words in the same order as you gave them, reading them together, and suggesting that the students write the words.

Then they can practice at home all four skills: listening, speaking, reading, and writing.

A paper.

A red (blue) paper.

Pick up a red (blue) paper.

Put a red (blue) paper on the table.

If beginning students have never written before or have other than Roman characters in their native language, reading and writing even the words they have understood and said may be difficult. Having the words they've just learned written on cards may be helpful. If they read and write in their own language, they may want to write the words phonetically in their own language to help them remember the correct pronunciation.

When starting a new lesson, always review the skills learned in the previous lesson. Then go on to new vocabulary.

Give me a blue (red, black, yellow) paper.

Point to a blue (red, black, yellow) paper.

Touch a blue (red, black, yellow) paper.

Continue manipulating these patterns until you are sure your students understand all the words. Your students may be concentrating so hard on following directions that they confuse the colors. Be patient. Go only as fast as is comfortable for the students. Reassure the students with verbal praise and a warm smile. During this exercise, they've learned colors, some commands and directions, and some reading and writing. This is an excellent ice-breaker for students who can speak no English at all. Confidence can be built up quickly because it requires active response rather than passive listening.

But what about more advanced students? You can use colored-paper exercises with any level students by including more complex commands for them to follow. The following commands can be quite complicated:

Pick up three green papers and put down two red papers.

Put two blue papers in the box, give me four red papers, and keep one red paper yourself.

Hold all the red papers in your left hand, but pick up the yellow papers with your right hand. Put a red paper between a blue and yellow paper, and put a black paper under them all.

You can teach the concepts of size (longer, shorter, larger, smaller), position (on, under, next to, etc.), or distance (e.g., two steps, across the room) through listening tasks. Later, encourage students to speak the sentences they've heard and understood, followed by reading and writing. Much practice will be needed. You might want to use colored pencils or crayons instead of papers, or pieces of colored yarn or string, or even colored toothpicks. Whatever medium you use, know that you can teach concepts in English with any readily available material, using controlled vocabulary at first, and expanding it as needed. Although exercises like these are useful for reinforcing certain skills, most of the lesson time should focus on real communication needs.

Role-Playing/Skits

In planning your lessons, you and your students will want to think together about the everyday situations that your students face. With the use of a few props, you can act out ordinary situations with your students.

Ask your students what they need to say in English. Where do they use English? Many situations, including the following, will probably come to mind:

- answering the telephone

- asking directions

- shopping in various kinds of stores

- telling a doctor about pain or illness

- ordering in a restaurant

- visiting a friend

- cashing a check at a bank

- making a recommendation at work

Most people will find statements and questions involving food items of immediate use. Although students may know some of the words, they may be pronouncing them incorrectly. Bring in food ads with prices from local papers. Set up a demonstration with a few items and act out a grocery shopping situation. Refer to the lists in *The Competency-Based Mainstream English Language Training (MELT)* in Appendix C for more topics incorporating real-life language skills that adult students may need.

To use the information in the lists most advantageously, look through them and compare the suggestions of topics and competency areas with your students' needs and skill levels. Choose activities that will introduce a topic and develop it so that it becomes part of your students' language skills. Note that each list progresses within each topic from the simplest needed listening comprehension to more complex conversation production.

Planned dialogues in role-playing situations can prepare students for real experiences. Spontaneous conversations are easier when specific topics of conversation have been identified. Many of us are "hams," enjoying acting and pretending. Try a little skit just for fun. You and your students might write a short skit with specific parts for each person. There are books available with short dramas that stress specific skills and are geared to ESOL students. Before you give them each a copy, read aloud the entire play or skit, acting it out yourself. Check that they understood first. Then have them read or role-play the parts.

The first skit one tutor used with a small group was "Fly Soup" (Hines, 1980), a two-page skit about a man in a restaurant who insisted that there was a fly in his soup. The ending was a surprise when it was found that the man had a box of flies in his pocket, obviously getting free meals by dropping them into the food after he'd eaten most of it. The students loved it, getting more dramatic each time they reread and re-acted the skit. Taping the third rehearsal gave them an opportunity to hear themselves and to laugh again. They didn't realize they were arguing, expressing curiosity, using the present tense—all objectives of this little drama.

One group of young mothers was concerned about visiting the doctor with their children. They enacted a visit to the doctor, which included making an appointment, arriving and talking to the nurse, asking the doctor questions, and reprimanding the children when necessary. This activity made the mothers feel more comfortable going into a real-life situation.

Problem Posing/Solving

Problem posing is associated with Paulo Freire (1970) in his effort to link literacy with critical political and social concerns that emerging readers face. A prevailing theme of his work is the ability to "read the word" in order to "read the world." Elsa Auerbach (1992) and Andrea Nash and her colleagues (Nash, Carson, Rhum, McGrail, and Gomez-Sanford, 1992) have expanded on Freire's ideas and have applied them within a context of ESOL instruction. Their work may be consulted to obtain ideas on linking language learning with some of the broader social and political issues that ESOL students face. See the bibliography for titles.

Problem posing and solving can be an entree into helping your students with their personal real-life situations. Problem posing is closely aligned with role-playing, for in both activities the students take the leading roles, acting out and talking about situations that are occurring in their daily lives. Encourage the students to bring in their own or imaginary problems with alternative suggestions for solving them. You, too, can bring in problems that you foresee could happen to them. Oral/aural language is used initially—listening to the problem, then paraphrasing, and finally suggesting possible solutions. Reading and writing can follow.

> *Victor Lifshits was trained as a nurse in Russia, but he found that his Russian credentials were not accepted by American hospitals. He worked as a maintenance worker in a local hospital, and, after observing the nursing procedures, he felt that his skills were more than adequate. He realized that he must improve his English first, but he was unsure what to do next.*

Victor shared his problem with the members of his small ESOL group. They listened attentively, thinking that eventually Victor should be given an opportunity to use his nursing skills in America. They wondered, "How can we help?"

They suggested that Victor contact the admissions office of the local nursing school, submitting his Russian credentials and giving evidence of his efforts to improve his English. They even worked as a group to draft a cover letter. Victor was elated, feeling his confidence boosted. Ensuring Victor's success would now be a project for the entire class.

Personal problems can be posed, or more general problems can be discussed. For example, what should a parent do when a school-age child is sick and both parents have full-time jobs? In many other countries, the grandparents look after such children. What should they do in America? Pictures can serve as catalysts for discussing some of the problems that your students face.

Jane Vella (1994) suggests using open-ended questions when posing problems to learners:

1. *What do you see happening here?* (description)

2. *Why do you think it is happening?* (analysis)

3. *When it happens in your situation, what problems does it cause?* (application)

4. *What can we do about it?* (implementation)

These questions will probably promote discussion of the issue, which will finally focus around alternatives and possible solutions.

The tutor and members of a small group are not expected to be counselors. They are not expected to solve all problems. However, they can listen well and be facilitators. Tutors can, through discussion, let students know that they care, and help them come up with some suggestions for solutions.

Field Trips

You may wish to make group trips to a grocery store, a restaurant, a museum, a park, or any other place relevant to your students. Your students will be given opportunities to hear other voices speaking English with you as support. Have them take notes, tape other voices, make a personal word list, take pictures—all can lead to class discussion and writing.

Picture Stories

Words tell stories; and so do pictures. There are commercial books with picture series that tell a story. Or you can use comic strips with the words deleted, or even make up your own using stick figures. Have the students look at all of the pictures. Then have them talk about the pictures, telling what they observe—what the characters are doing, where they are, what time of day or night it is,

From PULL - Project for Unique Learners in Literacy
Literacy Volunteers of America - Illinois 1994. Used by permission.

etc. Then have them tell you the story, following the sequence of the pictures. You write the story on the board or on paper and have them copy it. If the students are more advanced, they can write their own stories. It's fun to see how different people interpret the same pictures.

Music

Music is a wonderful bond between people as well as an excellent tool for helping students feel the rhythm of the new language and build vocabulary. Because they rhyme and are usually repetitive, songs can help develop pronunciation as well. Even if you can hardly carry a tune, you might want to try singing some well-known simple songs. For example, for beginning students you could sing "Row, Row, Row Your Boat"; for intermediate students "Three Blind Mice" is fun; and for more advanced students try singing the old campfire song, "Make New Friends." These will be good choices, especially for parents, since their children are likely to be learning songs like these in school. Have pictures available to help with comprehension. Sing the song through twice, having the students listen. Then have the students hum along, tapping the rhythm with a pencil on the table or clapping their hands.

You could bring in sing-along tapes or tapes of some traditional American songs, such as "Yankee Doodle," "Jingle Bells," "America the Beautiful," or "This Land Is Your Land." Or bring tapes from songs around the world that have been translated into English. Play the tape through, then together hum the melody along with the tape. Try inserting some of the words. You'll be surprised how many words the students can repeat. Do this several times, teaching the students the words as they go. Finally, give them a sheet with the words they have sung printed on it. Have them read the words, then sing them.

You can show the rhythm of English by having them say *la la la* to the tune even before they repeat the words. You can use this same exercise with nursery rhymes or even regular English sentences.

137

One tutor heard her Korean student humming "Amazing Grace" as she came to meet her. The tutor asked if she'd sing it for her in Korean. Quietly, in the corner of the local library, the student sang in Korean, and the tutor gradually joined along in English. The student said she wanted to learn to sing that song in English. There was no doubt where the rest of the lesson would be focused.

Several commercial books are available that show how to use music to teach English. Some songs use rhyming words with a steady beat, and others use non-rhyming words with an irregular beat, typical of much current music. There are many songs from which to choose.

Journals

As your students write more, encourage them to write daily in their own personal journals. They may or may not want to share these writings with you or other members of the group. This daily activity will not only give practice in writing skills, it can be used as a reference for areas where they want help. When trying to think of a real-life dialogue that they'd like to practice, they can refer to their journal, reminding themselves of times when they were at a loss for meaningful words.

Some students may want you to read their journals, responding to what they wrote. These dialogue or interactive journals will give you insight into your students' lives as well as an opportunity to see where they need help. You can use dialogue journals as a part of home assignments, or you can set aside perhaps ten minutes during the lesson for students to write in their journals. Those whose writing skills are limited can draw pictures or answer yes or no to your simple questions.

Comprehension Activities

One way to check comprehension is to have students follow directions or commands. Ask your students to do something. If they follow your directions, you know they understood you. You can do this with one student or with several. Ask the students to open the blue book to page 231. The students' listening level determines the difficulty of the instruction. For example, students with a low listening comprehension level could be expected to open the blue book, but not to a specific page.

Students with a higher level of listening comprehension could be asked to read silently the first sentence of the third paragraph and raise their hands when finished. Other students could be asked to read and then paraphrase specific sentences.

Bring a cake-mix box. Show the picture on the carton and read the directions. Have the students tell you, in sequence, what to do to bake a cake.

Asking questions is another way to check comprehension. *When, where, what, who, why,* and *how* questions can yield needed information as well as check how well your students understand.

> *When did you come to America? . . . did you get up?*
> *. . . did you leave for class?*
>
> *Where were you born? . . . do you live? . . . do you work?*
>
> *What do you like to do for recreation? . . . is your telephone number?*
>
> *Who do you know in America? . . . can you call for help ?*
>
> *Why do you need a car? . . . did your son miss school?*
>
> *How do you get to class? . . . do you spell your name?*

Asking questions at the completion of a reading, or even at the end of a lesson, tells you much about students' comprehension.

Holidays and Parties

You can always make an upcoming holiday the theme of several lessons, bringing in appropriate objects, pictures, decorations, and possibly songs.

Consider

New Year's Eve	Fourth of July
President's Day	Halloween
Easter	Thanksgiving
Memorial Day	Hanukkah
Dominion Day (Canadian)	Christmas
Boxing Day (Canadian)	Valentine's Day

Don't forget to have your students share holiday traditions from their native cultures. Members of a small group were discussing Memorial Day, America's day to commemorate its veterans who have died in battle, which reminded a woman from Japan of a Buddhist holiday. They decided they would go to a cemetery to honor and show respect to their dead relatives—and celebrate by having a picnic afterwards.

You might ask your students to share meaningful holidays in their countries. When discussing how Americans celebrate birthdays, an Indochinese student said that birthdays are not celebrated in his country. Birthday festivities are strange and new to many. One student from Vietnam told how the Vietnamese commemorate days of death as well as days of birth. Celebrating and explaining an American birthday party could open up a popular American tradition to many newcomers.

Potluck dinners or lunches with ESOL students can open doors to sharing foods of different countries. Suggest that each student bring some food native to his or her country. You might want to focus on one country at a time. For example, you might have a Polish day, when a Polish student brings one item of native food and tells about a holiday in Poland. The student given the limelight that day can speak in English about something familiar. The other students then get to listen to English being spoken by someone other than the tutor. The student could also teach a few Polish words to the group. This could be followed up by a written thank-you letter that the group sends to the student presenter.

Students' Interests

Be aware of your students' interests and needs. One tutor saw that her student had an ad for a refrigerator on her desk. She found that the student needed a new refrigerator and wanted help finding a good one. The other students in her small group agreed that this would be a good project. Their home assignment was to find out all they could about refrigerators. The tutor did the same.

Wonderful, lively conversation brought out much needed information. By examining different ads, they were doing comparison shopping. Some students wanted to know whether they could bargain, as they had done in their country. How much more would it cost if they didn't have all the money right then? They debated whether it was worthwhile to wait and save the money rather than make interest payments.

Ask your students what they want to discuss. You can choose lesson topics according to their interests. Once they decide on a topic, you bring in props, but also ask the students to bring in props. Gardening, buying a car, sports, travels, family activities—the list is endless for a focus of a lesson.

Don't forget that *National Geographic* magazines contain colorful pictures of scenes from nearly every country. One student, upon seeing a picture of her country, actually cried. She was just bursting to tell the group more about her country. Before this, the tutor hadn't had much success with getting her to speak in English—she was too embarrassed. Seeing a familiar scene gave her the incentive to talk.

Free Conversation

Free and easy conversation that is interesting and informative is what you should strive for in your lessons. Keep the students talking. The key often is to find a topic of interest to start the conversation. Often a question or a request for the students to tell you about something can lead the way. There are suggested conversation starters in the appendix.

If you will stop, look, and listen to your own small social groups, you will note that some individuals tend to dominate the group (the talkers) while others sit back quietly (the listeners). This is natural in most groups and probably will happen even when you are tutoring only one student—that person could be shy and resist trying to talk, or adventuresome and willing to try new and difficult words. Individuals, whether alone with a tutor or in a small group, can be encouraged to become both talkers and listeners. This is the responsibility of the tutor and can be done through games as well as through free or directed conversation.

Technology

Using Tapes, TV, Radio

Encourage your students to bring their own tape recorders and cassette tapes to record whatever parts of lessons they want to review. They can then go over the lesson as many times as they wish at home, using you as a model for both pronunciation and rhythm.

It usually takes playing a new tape several times for most ESOL students to really understand its content well enough to paraphrase it. As your students progress, longer and longer portions of tapes may be used.

First playing	Ask simple *yes/no* questions as you check for comprehension.
Second playing	Ask open-ended questions, challenging the students to respond in their own words.
Third playing	Suggest that the students put in their own words what they heard.

You can always follow up by having them write what they heard.

Listening to the radio to get the news, sports, or weather reports gives excellent practice in developing listening skills. You might suggest you both listen to the same broadcast, perhaps the 6 o'clock news, and discuss it at the next lesson. Providing a brief chart to fill out can help students with comprehension. For example:

	TODAY	TOMORROW	DAY AFTER TOMORROW
High Temperature	82° (degrees)	85°	77°
Low Temperature	65°	62°	60°
Weather (cloudy, rainy, etc.)	sunshine	cloudy	rain

Many international students come to the United States for advanced degrees. They can read and write well in their chosen field, but they often have trouble understanding American lecturers in classrooms. Suggest they tape a lecture, playing it back later in small chunks. Encourage them to replay the tape as often as needed. You can play back portions of it in your sessions.

Libraries have many books on tape. Use matched tapes and books so that students can read along—hearing, seeing, and saying. Even advanced students who want to improve their listening skills can benefit from listening to different voices on tapes.

Using Computers

Computers are being used more and more for teaching reading and writing. Computers with sound capabilities enable students to hear words while they see corresponding words or pictures on the screen. You may want to check with your library or a local college or university regarding programs for learning computer skills or availability of educational computer programs that don't require much computer knowledge.

Games

Both you and your students will be putting much effort into learning new skills, but be sure to allot time for fun and relaxation. Games are a natural way to learn and reinforce learning.

Listening Games

Games can be fun as the students practice listening skills. Make bingo sheets. Instead of using numbers in the boxes, use pictures depicting words of minimal pairs of contrasting sounds that need reinforcement. If you're working on the /th/ and /t/ sounds, use pictures depicting words such as

thorn	*torn*
thread	*tread*
three	*tree*
thug	*tug*

For the /i/ and /ee/ sounds, you could use pictures depicting words such as

sit	*seat*
mitt	*meat*
fit	*feet*

You call out words and the students cover the pictures of them on the bingo sheets. The winners are those who correctly identify the pictures of the words they hear, in rows or columns or diagonally, just as in regular bingo. Later you can uncover the words on the bingo card, asking your students to read them.

Vocabulary Games

Use games to reinforce the skills taught in lessons. You can ask students to give the female or male counterparts of the following words:

boy-girl	*niece-nephew*
man-woman	*father-mother*
groom-bride	*brother-sister*
uncle-aunt	*son-daughter*
actor-actress	*waiter-waitress*

Or you might ask for plurals:

boy-boys	*girl-girls*
man-men	*woman-women*

You can use the same idea with opposites:

tall-short	*slow-fast*
up-down	*top-bottom*
old-young	*old-new*
fat-thin	*big-small*

Concentrate on regular patterns at first: the irregular ones can come later. Don't be surprised if the lesson doesn't go exactly as planned. One student gave *second-hand* as the opposite of *new*. This is, of course, a perfectly acceptable, and maybe even preferable, answer.

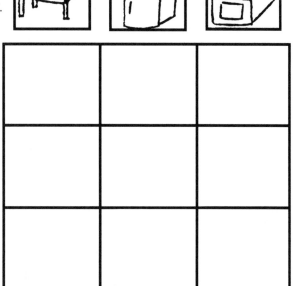

Here is another activity that reinforces listening comprehension and expands vocabulary. Decide on a specific topic for vocabulary building, such as kitchen items, garden plants, or parts of a car.

If your students want to know the vocabulary of kitchen items, make stick drawings of a table, a refrigerator, and a stove on small cards, or clip pictures from magazines, catalogues, etc. Block off a large sheet of paper as shown on the right.

Ask the students to put the refrigerator in the upper left-hand corner of the paper, the stove in the lower right-hand corner, the table in front of the stove, etc. Make sure your students know the meaning of *upper, left-hand, corner,* etc.

Another helpful activity for ESOL students is identifying the kinds of things one can buy at certain types of stores:

> *What do you buy at a . . . shoe store?*
>
> > *bakery?*
> >
> > *post office?*
>
> *What can you buy at a drug store that you cannot buy at any other store?*
>
> *Where can you buy fruit?*
>
> *Where can you get stamps?*

After your students are familiar with the names for colors, use them in real situations:

> *The traffic signals have __, __, and __ lights.*
>
> *Nurses wear __ uniforms.*
>
> *The colors of the American flag are __, __, and __.*
>
> *In traffic, a blinking __ light means proceed with caution or go slowly.*

Sometimes it is easier to learn new vocabulary words that have something in common. They're called "group words." You can make your own group words by bringing items from one category for fun and learning. If your students are interested in gardening, you might bring garden tools: a watering can, pruning shears, a weeder, a sprinkler, garden gloves, and so on. Another time you might bring articles having to do with an office: pen, paper clips, 3-hole paper punch, eraser, ruler, highlighter. Pictures often suggest natural groups of words.

Start the activity with a sentence describing how the articles are used or how they could be used in a sentence. One group was interested in cooking, and the tutor brought kitchen-related materials: knife, fork, spoon, bowl, cup, saucer, and several other basic kitchen items. It's reassuring if the tutor names and points to each item first. Then the tutor picks up the knife and says:

> *To make dinner, I need a knife.*

The first student picks up the knife, repeating the tutor's sentence, adding a second item, picking it up and naming it.

> *To make dinner, I need a knife and a bowl.*

Each student and the tutor continue until all the items have been named. Have the names of all the articles written down on 3" x 5" cards or on a piece of paper. The students can then read the new words and copy them for their own review.

For the next session the tutor asks the students to bring their own kitchen items for identification and the tutor brings more unusual kitchen tools: spatula, salt and pepper shakers, napkins, strainer, can opener. Some of the students know specific items and use them often but do not know the English word for them: *rolling pin, colander, double boiler, knife sharpener.* This is true collaboration: the students are participating in the lesson plans.

At one meeting, a Greek student brought in spanakopita. Everyone enjoyed it and wanted to know how she made it. This group adapted the group word game. Maria started by saying:

I made spanakopita. I used flour.

Maria listed the ingredients and each student had to say their names.

Maria made spanakopita. She used flour and water.

They included other ingredients: *feta cheese, spinach, eggs, pepper, onions, and butter.* The students listened first, then spoke. Later the students read Maria's recipe and copied it for themselves.

Conversation Games

As you try to engage the students in free conversation, it's surprising how one thing leads right into another.

> *We were enjoying strawberry shortcake. I said we really could brag about Alicia's strawberry shortcake. I saw eyebrows rise as I said brag. I explained, giving examples, and then each one was to brag about someone or something. It was revealing to hear students brag about their husband's work, their children's activities, their own cooking, their achievements at the university—being modest yet proud.*

There are hidden talents in every person and in every group. One student was a baker and invited his tutor to his home where he gave him a baking lesson. Another student showed how to quilt a pillow. Another planted a miniature garden. As these students showed their special skills, they talked. That's conversational English. Pictures can always be used to generate and focus conversation. Use whatever you can to encourage students to talk.

A good conversation game is Twenty Questions. One person mentally picks out an object in the room or a well-known place or person. The others take turns asking up to twenty questions that can be answered by yes or no, trying to identify the object, place, or person. The person who guesses it correctly gets the opportunity to choose another object, place, or person.

You can add new vocabulary words by bringing in a special object from another country or something unique. Whatever it is, it becomes the focus of conversation. Have a variety of questions ready, soliciting discussion in English.

What do you think this is?

What's it made of?

What's it used for?

Where do you think it was made?

Do you have one?

Would you like one?

Once the students see how it is done, they are often willing to bring in objects from their countries. They then become the leaders and ask similar questions.

Be alert to ways you can use new words from the students' conversations, explaining them when necessary, and then letting the students carry their ideas further. Once I was discussing with a small group of students how individuals felt when they first came to America. Johanna from Zaire in Central Africa had never seen snow or felt such cold when she arrived in Syracuse in midwinter. In her limited English, Johanna explained that she was confined to her small apartment. She said she was in a . . . . She groped for the right word. With gestures she made bars at the window. We understood. *Prison,* someone said. That opened the conversation to more vocabulary: *prisoner, thieves, judge, lawyer, fine,* and *speeding.*

Show and Tell gives individual students an opportunity to share. One student showed colored slides of her country. In her enthusiasm of sharing her country with us she forgot her embarrassment about her poor English. Another brought objects from her country, describing them and their uses. Putting a student in the limelight with familiar subjects helps build pride and confidence.

Communication Games

An information gap activity is a communication game in which some people know something that the others don't, and they must communicate in order to solve a problem or complete a puzzle. The following is a communication game that two people can play. Player A and Player B sit back-to-back. Similar small objects or pictures are in front of each, plus paper and pen. Player A tells Player B to draw something or to move one of the objects or pictures to a certain spot. Player A could say:

Put the paper between pages 23 and 24 of the book.

Draw a circle at the bottom of the page.

Fold the paper in half.

Put the paper clip on page 12.

After six or seven directives, have the players compare what they've done. If the results are the same, Player B understood Player A. Even if there are differences, they are likely to have had a good time and to have learned as well.

Another communication game can be played by several people. Several objects are placed in front of the group. One player describes one object or picture. The other players try to identify the object or picture described. If some of the objects and pictures are similar, the game is more difficult. The only restrictions are that the person describing the object must use English, and the identifier must listen and identify that object in English, not merely point to it.

Some ESOL students with traditional educational backgrounds may think games are only for children. It may be useful to point out to parents in the group that by learning new games, they can teach them to their children. Of course, there are many adult games like Scrabble and Monopoly that your students may well enjoy. When introducing these games, be sensitive to your students' reactions. Some students may enjoy playing games; others may not.

There are many books describing games and activities for English-language learning. Remember that in working with ESOL students, hard-and-fast rules rarely apply. ESOL students come from all over the world and represent many different ages, educational and vocational backgrounds, and general life experiences. No two students will fit into the same mold, and you will want to adapt any game to the interests of your particular students.

SUMMARY

Once you've learned and practiced various techniques and exercises for teaching English to Speakers of Other Languages, it's rewarding and fun to apply them to the everyday needs of your students. The resources and activities described in this chapter are only the beginning. You'll encounter other activities in books, journals, and in other workshops. But don't hesitate to create your own resources and activities as well. Do share those that you find helpful and fun for your students with other tutors in your local program. Also, feel free to send any ideas to LVA.

GOALS AND LESSON PLANS

CHAPTER

IX

- ♦ IMPORTANCE OF STUDENTS' GOALS
- ♦ PLANNING TOGETHER
- ♦ LESSON PLANS PLANNING CHART
- ♦ SUMMARY

CHAPTER IX
GOALS AND LESSON PLANS

IMPORTANCE OF STUDENTS' GOALS

Every student has a goal in mind when asking for help to learn English. Sometimes these goals may take a long time to achieve. One ESOL student may wish to become a computer programmer. Still another may want to pass a high school equivalency exam. Another student may want to gain confidence in listening and speaking skills in order to attend parent-teacher conferences or to participate in the school parent-teacher organization.

These are long-term goals. Such goals are desirable and should be encouraged. However, it is difficult to develop lessons on a daily or weekly basis with only long-term goals in mind. From these long-term goals, short-term goals can be identified with objectives that can be attained daily, weekly, or monthly.

A beginning student's first short-term goal may be to be able to understand and respond to simple greetings in English. Another student may want to learn enough survival vocabulary to do weekly grocery shopping or to make an appointment with a doctor. Some of your lesson planning should focus on the more immediate needs of your students, but you should also keep your students' longer-range goals and objectives in mind as you plan lessons. Both short-term and long-term goals may be revised as you and your students progress together.

As you make your lesson plans, keep in mind who your students are and how you can help them address their real-life concerns. Adapt techniques, exercises, and activities so they relate to the interests of your students. For example, if one student has expressed feelings of loneliness and isolation, consider how you could bring these issues before your small group as part of your instructional program. You might read aloud a story of someone in a similar situation, asking the students not only to paraphrase the story, but to suggest other ways a lonely newcomer could fit into his or her new community.

Literacy Volunteers of America, Inc.

PLANNING TOGETHER

Planning for individual lessons is mainly your responsibility, but it should involve the students as much as possible.

As you plan, keep the following in mind:

1. Assessment. Find out

- where your students use English now with relative ease
- where they have difficulty with English now
- where they will need to use English in the future
- what their strengths and weaknesses with English are
- what their interests are
- what they want to accomplish

Review the results of the *ESLOA* or other assessment tools as well as the continuing assessment done in individual students' portfolios and the *ESLOA: Level Description Grid*.

2. Teaching. Incorporate listening, speaking, reading, and writing while maintaining a balanced Communicative Approach; vary the activities and resources used as you focus on both authentic materials and real-life situations.

3. Reinforcement. Review and reteach, giving suggestions for using the newly acquired skills outside of lesson time.

4. Evaluation. You and your students should answer the following questions:

- Have we done what we set out to do?
- Are the students improving their English skills?
- Are the lessons focused on the students' needs?
- Are the students eager and contributing?

The first cycle of planning becomes complete when you and the students go back to assessment as you plan for continuing lessons.

LESSON PLANS

You may have wonderful lesson plans prepared, but you should always be ready to adapt them to students' immediate concerns. Lists of suggested topics for learner-centered curricula for each level student are included in the *ESLOA User's Guide*. Other suggested topics are in the *MELT* list in Appendix C.

It is difficult to plan a lesson until you have specific students in mind and know about their abilities and interests. When you are actually working with students, you can tailor your lesson plans to their real needs and goals. Making realistic lesson plans is an important part of your teaching. Knowing what you are going to do and how you plan to do it will give you confidence, eliminating that *What will I do next?* feeling. Your confidence will spread to your students. That's one reason why preparation is so important. The more self-assured you are as a teacher, the more reassured your students will feel.

Planning allows you to be more flexible and more creative. It is better to plan more than you can use rather than not enough. Plan some easy activities and some more challenging ones. Plan some that are short, others that will take longer. Vary the pace in your lessons. Every lesson should be interesting and challenging but never frustrating.

Lesson plans can be as simple or as complex as you want. You can use a spiral or loose-leaf notebook, putting specific things to be done on the left page, and using the right page for your own comments. Or you can simply draw a line down the center of a page, using the left half for your lesson plans, the right half for your comments.

SAMPLE LESSON PLAN

Date:_____ Student's name or group name:_____

Goal (simple statement of what you want to do):

Objectives (simple statement of what you'll do to get there):

Materials needed:

Warm-up:

Review of homework:

Review of last week's work:

New material:

Questions and comments:

Evaluation:

Assignment of homework:

Ending:

The goal for a lesson could be *to be able to say and understand the vocabulary needed to buy a used car.* The objective could be as simple as *learn appropriate vocabulary; act out a dialogue for buying a used car.* In the lesson plan, list the specific exercises and activities you plan on doing. This will help alert you to materials you might need.

Warm-up Reception

You can vary the way you open your lessons, but if your students know that you will start on time, they will usually make an effort to be on time. For a small group, simple chain drills are fun. You might review greetings in English, varying the words by using different situations. Show a picture of two teenage friends meeting. Their greeting could be *Hi,* slapping each others' palms high-five fashion. Going into a doctor's office or a car salesroom would suggest a more formal greeting of *Good afternoon* or *Good morning.* Your students might suggest other situations where they would like to know how Americans greet each other.

Homework Assignments Review

Two or three hours a week of tutoring is only a part of language learning. English must be used in order to be learned. Show that you really are interested in the assignments your students did. If students completed written assignments, you might ask them to volunteer to read them aloud or just hand them in so that you can review their work later. If they were to listen to a specific news broadcast, you might want to discuss what they heard. Don't be surprised if, in spite of great intentions, some students don't have the time or the inclination to do the assigned homework. Remember, they are adults and usually have lots of responsibilities and full, active lives outside the tutoring session. They are not neglectful if they don't do their home assignments. They are merely working at a pace that is comfortable for them. They are putting their language lessons in the context of their lives and priorities.

Last Session's Work Review

A review of the work done during the last session where there was success helps build the students' confidence. A review of work accomplished prepares them for accepting the challenge of new work. It is especially important to review last session's work if it relates to the current session.

New Material

When presenting new material, remember to balance all four language skills. You should first have the students listen to the new material, then have them speak, either repeating or paraphrasing what you said or read to them. Invite them to read the same selection, either to themselves or aloud. Then have them write. Sometimes you may want to vary this. Students might write something, then read it aloud so the group can discuss what they have heard. New material could be as simple as new words using colored paper exercises or free conversation on any given subject, depending on the competency level of your students and their goals and needs.

Introduce new material early in the lesson while the students are fresh. If the students want to learn the vocabulary necessary to buy a car, you will have prepared some suggested *group words*. They could be the brands of some of the cars your students express interest in buying, such as *Ford, Chevrolet, Honda.*

If you have ads for used cars, you will find many pertinent words: *lease, time plans, interest, color, interior, engine, mileage.* After you read the ads aloud to your students, ask them which words are new to them.

You might want to have them memorize a dialogue to make them more comfortable on their first shopping trip.

Salesperson:	Good afternoon. May I help you?
Student:	Yes, thank you. I'm looking for a used car. I don't have much money so, it must be inexpensive.
Salesperson:	Did you have something specific in mind?
Student:	Yes, I saw your ad for a 1987 Ford.

A lesson on buying a used car could be the main topic for several sessions. You might even want take the group to a used car lot.

A game could be included in this part of your lesson, or you could use a game later as reinforcement. Vary the activities, resources, books, and pictures you use.

Home Assignment

You have watched the time, and you note that you have only ten minutes left. This is just enough time to give specific home assignments. When you meet with your students for the first time, it's important to ask them how much time they can devote to homework assignments. Don't give more than they can reasonably do in the amount of time they have available. Learning English is not a marathon. Go at the students' pace. If some students have more free time, give those students more to do at home.

Language skills must be practiced to be acquired and maintained. No one learns a language without practice, and it is the students who are in charge of how much they practice. Anyone who suggests that a new language can be learned during lesson time alone raises false hopes and wastes the time of both the tutor and the students. Students must practice every day.

You can always suggest reading and writing assignments. But how can beginning students practice their listening and speaking skills without the tutor present?

- Encourage your students to listen to spoken English—on TV and radio, in groups, in the family—even if the student doesn't fully understand. Surrounding themselves with English will help them get a feel for its rhythm.

153

- If your students have access to tape recorders, record stories to be listened to and exercises to be practiced.

- Give your students a folder, envelope, or notebook for study materials. The students can repeat some of the activities alone or get an English-speaking friend or member of the family to help.

  The folder might include

  ▶ colored pieces of paper

  ▶ numbers and letters on index cards

  ▶ stick-figure cards

  ▶ pictures

  ▶ written words from the lesson

- Assign a simple task to perform (e.g., asking in English for the time, or saying an address or an English name written on a piece of paper).

  Homework assignments for a more advanced student could include:

  ▶ participating in English-speaking groups, urging the students to speak even if their English is limited

  ▶ listening to a specific TV or radio broadcast, knowing the tutor and other students will discuss it at the following lesson

  ▶ discussing a picture with a friend, or writing a few sentences about it

  ▶ practicing a written dialogue from a lesson

  ▶ repeating taped sentences

  ▶ reviewing a taped story

  ▶ performing a special task (e.g., calling directory assistance for a certain number; asking someone in a store or on the street for directions)

```
┌─────────────────────────────────────────────────────────────────────────┐
│                     SUGGESTIONS FOR LESSON PLANS                          │
│                                                                           │
│  Student's Name_____ Time_____ Date____   Levels III and IV             │
│                                                                           │
│                                             1. Conversation: Encourage    │
│  Levels I and II                            your student to share recent  │
│                                             experiences and to ask you    │
│  1. Greeting.                               questions. You can check      │
│                                             pronunciation and structure   │
│  2. Listening comprehension.                in this free conversation     │
│     (1) Commands — Directions: stand        time.                         │
│     up, sit down, etc.                                                    │
│     (2) Colored paper exercises.            2. Review homework: Find out   │
│                                             what was incompletely learned │
│  3. Vocabulary, using:                      in order to give additional   │
│     (1) Substitution drill and response     practice. Your student will   │
│     drill.                                  welcome drill in difficult    │
│     (2) Objects.                            areas.                        │
│     (3) Pictures without words.                                           │
│                                             3. New material: Listening    │
│  4. Survival skills.                        comprehension, vocabulary and │
│                                             speaking skills, reading and  │
│  5. Textbooks, e.g. chapters on plurals,    writing, using:               │
│  negatives, etc.                               (1) Pictures.              │
│                                                (2) Textbooks.             │
│  6. Simple dialogue.                           (3) Reading books.         │
│                                                (4) Tape recorder.         │
│  7. Fun: pictures of your family, with         (5) Dialogue.              │
│  simple descriptions; your student's                                      │
│  country, giving the student something      4. Relaxing activities for    │
│  familiar to discuss, etc.                  fun and reinforcement: games, │
│                                             reading a story together, or  │
│  8. Tutor: Review this lesson, writing      tutor reading a story which   │
│  down your comments as a guide to           student can re-tell.          │
│  planning the next lesson.                                                │
│                                             5. Homework assigned.         │
│                                                                           │
│                                             6. Tutor: Review this lesson, │
│                                             writing your comments as a    │
│                                             guide to planning the next    │
│                                             lesson.                       │
└─────────────────────────────────────────────────────────────────────────┘
```

Questions and Comments

Near the end of each session, both you and your students can start to wind down. The work part of the lesson is over and home assignments have been given. Encourage your students to ask questions, to give feedback on what they felt really was helpful and where they would like more help. This time assures the students that their feelings and their input are important. Note their comments on your lesson plan sheet.

Stories in English for Pleasure

The last five minutes of your lesson should be relaxing. Learning new material in a new language can be very tiring, and it's important to end the session with something that is fun. If you have beginning students, you might want to share family or magazine pictures.

As soon as you know your students understand some English, tell in your own words or read aloud to them a short story in English. Show the pictures from the book first, telling them what the story will be about. You might want to talk or read more slowly than normal here. Let them enjoy the story. Don't ask for their input. This is purely for their relaxation and enjoyment; language learning doesn't always have to be work. They will be hearing the flow of English and picking up new vocabulary as well.

Joint Summations

You might end a session by asking your students to write a few sentences in their journals. You can use that time to write as well, summing up the day's lesson, what the students have learned, what still needs to be worked on, and what ideas can be used in future lessons.

PLANNING CHART

It's not important for beginning ESOL students to know rules about language. It is important that they use the English they know. In using a new language, people make errors and these errors are actually steps in the learning process.

A planning chart can be of real help in lesson planning. Rather than interrupting the lesson constantly to correct your student, jot down special problems to return to later. You may notice a pattern of pronunciation problems. Sometimes you will want to help your student immediately by modeling correctly, but often you may prefer to work on errors in future lessons.

PLANNING CHART

Error	Needs Help	Completed
Says *shocks* for *socks*, *shun* for *sun*	Work on /s/ sound.	
Confuses *bit* and *beet*	Work on words that sound alike (minimal pair exercises)	
Doesn't understand difference between hospital and clinic.	Work on comprehension between doctor meanings	

NOTES AND NEW LESSON PLANS

You will save yourself a great deal of time and do a much better job if you jot down your comments and suggestions immediately after each lesson, while the completed lesson is fresh in your mind. With your materials at hand, you can plan quickly and easily. If you need additional new materials, write a note to yourself and attend to it immediately. The habit of planning the next lesson immediately pays big dividends. You might want to use the following simple format or develop one of your own:

A MODEL LESSON PLAN FORMAT		
Student's Name_____Date_____		
Plans	**Done**	**Next Time**
Review		
New Material		
Home Assignment		
Read for Enjoyment		
Comments		

MORE ON LESSON PLANS

While seeking to vary the lessons, do not neglect repetition. The importance of repetition to learning a new language cannot be overstressed. Since learning requires unconscious assimilation before it becomes natural, students need to hear and say words, phrases, and sentences many times and in many contexts before they can use them automatically.

Integrate new material immediately and begin to expand its context. For example, if you are teaching or reviewing numbers in English, your students can progress from simple arithmetic to reading prices, telling time, and giving change in American money. You might even go with or take them to a nearby store where they can actually find prices, purchase something, pay for it, and count their change to be sure it's correct. Help your students realize that what they are learning has many practical applications. Using material in many different ways gives you an opportunity for repetition and review.

To encourage your students to think in English, get them personally invested in activities: Have them follow directions or add a sentence to a story you have started. In such activities, if done with few pauses, there will be no time for translation from the students' native languages to English. The object is to get the students to think in English, so don't stop to correct errors. Make notes about errors for later lessons in your planning chart.

When you are working with one student, lesson plans seem to come more easily because you get to know your student well. You know the student's capabilities and needs, and can project them into lesson plans. Working together is a dialogue, for there are only two of you. However, when working with several students in a small group, keep in mind that you want to include all the students in activities. Realize that your plans should include the following:

- some activities where the entire group works together, even repeating or speaking chorally as a group

- some activities where students work in pairs, practicing techniques and exercises, working on a joint project, or perhaps just talking together

- a time when the group watches a movie or listens to a tape, a student presenter, or the tutor

- some quiet time when students work on writing activities

A balanced lesson that includes everyone is a satisfying lesson.

Knowing techniques and exercises thoroughly will help you adapt to individual student's needs whether you have one student or a group of students.

Literacy Volunteers of America, Inc.

SUMMARY

Your goal is to help your students reach their goals. By making lesson plans ahead of time, you'll help your students reach those goals more quickly. While you can always be flexible and adapt, it's a comfortable feeling to know that you have that plan in front of you. Both you and your students will relax and enjoy the lessons more.

CHAPTER

X

- ◆ **THE FIRST LESSON**

- ◆ **ONGOING LESSONS**

- ◆ **EXAMPLES OF LESSONS IN EACH OF FOUR LEVELS**

- ◆ **SUMMARY**

CHAPTER X
YOUR SESSIONS TOGETHER

THE FIRST LESSON

If your students have not been tested before being assigned, you won't know how well your students can speak, understand, read, or write English. For the first lesson you must have several potential lesson plans so that you can adapt the lesson to the students. However, even at the very first lesson you can bring your "bag of tricks" with you and give your students appropriate tasks geared to their abilities. This bag of tricks might include

- information about your students: names, addresses, telephone numbers, native countries, levels of education, etc.

- *I Speak English*

- *ESLOA (the English as a Second Language Oral Assessment)*

- notebooks, pens, portfolio folders

- bilingual dictionary

- sample textbook

- student Survival Kit (See Chapter VIII)

- objects for simple drills, exercises, or activities

- colored paper strips

- picture file, travel magazines, etc.

- your name, address, and phone number to give to students

Keep your materials in a bag. The important thing is to keep them together and ready to go.

Place, Time, Introductions

You and your students have been notified of when and where to meet. If you are a bit nervous, know that your students are probably even more so.

The first session with your students is important because you are setting the climate for future meetings. Don't let your desire to be friendly make you too effusive. Have a name tag for yourself as well as for each student.

As each student enters, speak distinctly as you introduce yourself, saying simply,

> *Hello, my name is . . .*

Some students may respond with *Hello* and give their names. To the student who merely smiles, you could ask,

> *What's your name?*

If there is still no response, you know that the student probably doesn't understand any English and cannot even respond with his or her name. Start right there.

Point to the student and say his or her name. Point to yourself as you say your own name. Repeat this procedure to make sure the student understands. Then point to yourself and say,

> *My name is . . .*

Then point to the student, inserting his or her name, saying,

> *My name is . . .,*

gesturing for the student to repeat. You say *my* when saying your student's name because your student will be repeating your exact words. In practice, this procedure is not confusing. Most students will catch on quickly. Generally the students will want to be able to introduce themselves and will welcome the chance to learn how to say the introductions correctly.

The first session will be a "get acquainted" session and a time to begin to learn what the language needs of your students are. Your students will be looking you over, wondering how tutoring will work out. You will be assessing your students' abilities—strengths and weaknesses—and striving to build up the confidence you both need. As you make plans for your next meeting, be sure to write down the date and time. You might make copies of pages of a calendar, jotting down the date and time of the next lesson. If any students cannot read, you can suggest that perhaps a friend or family member will help.

A friendly *Hello* and *Good-bye* in English can begin and end each session, but you might want to learn the greetings in your students' languages. You would then have a taste of a new language and would certainly put your students at ease by sharing an interest in their language, too.

If you have more than one student, you might want to try the introductory chain drill, learning each other's names and perhaps their native countries. The first time:

Hi, I'm _____, and I'm from _____.

Later:

Hi, this is _____, and he's from _____.

I'm _____, and I'm from _____.

Assessment

You have probably been given a general assessment of your students, perhaps a level in the *ESLOA* and a note telling you of their native countries and general educational background. If not, you may want to consider giving them the *ESLOA* or using another assessment tool near the end of this first session or early in the next session. You will need a base from which you can start your planning.

Know that assessment will be ongoing. You may want to give each student a folder or envelope in which to keep work organized. You should also have a folder for each student. Your assessment starts at your first session together.

Preview Your General Plans

If your students speak and understand no English, you can start with beginning techniques and exercises. However, if your students speak and understand some English, you need to ask them what they want to learn and to tell them a bit of what you expect to do together.

You will have included in your materials some ESOL books, some pictures, and your own survival kit. Displaying them on the table gives even beginning students an idea of some of the activities you have planned. Encourage them to look over the items, taking note of what seems to be of interest to them.

You might want to suggest certain basic rules, such as *no smoking during lessons* or *call if you cannot attend a lesson.* Give each of them your phone number to keep in their portfolios. You might even discuss homework, telling them the importance of out-of-class work.

The Lesson

It is crucial that each student learn at least one needed thing, even in the first lesson. It might be their address, phone number, or how to use a phone book or read a bus schedule. Because you aren't sure of the abilities of these new students, you should have several plans in mind. If the students are beginners, you might try the colored-paper exercises. If they are more advanced, you might talk together about a picture you have brought. You might even introduce a dialogue to be memorized.

Don't try to do too much in that first lesson because it might frustrate the students. Remember, the first lesson is a get-acquainted lesson.

Closing

End the lesson promptly or even a few minutes early. Ask if there are any questions. Remind them of the next meeting and give a simple way to say good-bye. It could be as simple as:

Good-bye, I'll see you on Thursday.

Encourage them to repeat the words. Next session you can build on that.

After you end the session, stay just a few minutes longer so you can jot down what you did and what you learned about each student, putting those comments in each individual portfolio. It is easier to do it immediately after the lesson, when things are fresh in your mind. From those notes you can quickly make a new lesson plan for the next session.

ONGOING LESSONS

General Plans

Once you are in the habit of making lesson plans immediately after each session, you can quickly pull together the material you need—pictures, tape recorder, textbooks, etc. You then have no worries about *What will I do?* because you have your plans ready. You might want to review Chapter IX, *Goals and Lesson Plans,* as well as the various techniques, exercises, resources, and activities suggested in other parts of the book.

If Things Don't Go as Planned

Even the best-laid plans can't always be adhered to, so you must be adaptable. If you have had good training and rely on this book as a constant companion, you should have no troubles.

Your students will understand—in fact, they may feel more confident if they know that you aren't perfect. So when things don't go exactly as planned, just relax, laugh, and explain that you, too, will have to do more homework to adjust to new situations. The more experience you gain as a tutor, the more answers you will have to questions and new situations that come up.

You can always call your affiliate office for help and suggestions. There are probably in-service trainings you can attend. Join as many "help" groups as you can. Life is indeed a series of learning experiences, and this training and your new teaching experience can be valuable ones.

Portfolio Assessment

As you add to each student's portfolio, keep in mind that you will want to set times to review portfolios with individual students. It is helpful to set at least a half-hour aside for each student perhaps once every eight to ten weeks. This will help you and your students actually see the progress they are making. You might want to update the *ESLOA: Level Description Grid* at this time. You could choose to do assessment at a time when students are feeling frustrated, as it will encourage them to see their undeniable progress.

EXAMPLES OF LESSONS IN EACH OF THE FOUR LEVELS

Plans for Lessons

In all lessons it is useful to include elements of the four communication skills—listening, speaking, reading, and writing. The specifics will differ depending on the level of your students, what they want to learn, and what types of material are used. The following takes you through the same general content objective to provide you with a sense of the progression of complexity for each level. They are not lesson plans in the strict sense, with timed sequences for instructional activities. Rather, they illustrate how to integrate language skills for a given topic and show the developmental complexity of lessons. They are based upon a student's language level. Use the sample lessons as a model or a framework as you begin planning with and for your own students.

Sample Lesson Plan Suggestions for Level I Students

Content Objective: Shopping at the Market for Food

- Work with pictures of food items that you bring in or use from the *Basic New Oxford Picture Dictionary*.

- Have students make a shopping list from the pictures. Limit it to a few items.

- Practice listening comprehension by showing the pictures and saying the names of the food items.

- Point to the pictures and ask the students to say the food items. Include repetition.

- Make flashcards of the words ahead of time and ask the students to read them.

- Ask students to write the words on the backs of the pictures.

- Practice the substitution drill: *I want to buy some _____.*

- Make plans to go to the market with the students at a later date and point out the names of important food items.

- Point out the differences in prices of different brands.

Sample Lesson Plan Suggestions for Level II Students

Content Objective: Shopping at the Market for Food

- Work with pictures of food items from the regular *New Oxford Picture Dictionary*.

- Practice listening comprehension by showing the pictures, saying the names of the food items, and making up a short sentence about each food or group of food items.

- Have students make a shopping list from the pictures. Group the list according to food type.

- Ask students to make flashcards of food items, and on the back note the food type to which it belongs.

- Ask students to cut coupons out of the newspaper you have brought and have them sort the coupons according to food category and item.

- Read and discuss with students the contents of the coupons.

- Practice simple and complex substitution drills, e.g., *Harold bought lettuce, tomatoes, and carrots to make a salad. Martha bought wine, steak, potatoes, and French bread to prepare a special meal.*

- Make plans to go to the market with the students later, pointing out names of food items, comparing prices of different brands, and figuring out the final prices after using coupons.

Sample Lesson Plan Suggestions for Level III Students

Content Objective: Shopping at the Market for Food

- Discuss with students what they need help with in food shopping. Possible topics may include "stretching" dollars, comparison shopping, or assessing nutritional value of food items.

- Have students make a list of essential and nonessential items that they would purchase in preparation for a major shopping trip.

- Have students cut out coupons in the newspaper in preparation for the trip. Discuss the potential value of the coupons and make sure that your students understand all the fine-print details.

- Bring in canned or boxed food items of varying sizes and discuss nutritional information with your students.

- Bring in a general text on nutrition to help them make appropriate food selections. Read it to your students to stimulate discussion.

- Discuss and plan possible meal selections for the week that would help them organize shopping, discussing the amounts of money required. Ask your students to create a meal list for the week.

- Go to the market together, working with the list, budget, and coupons. Do comparison shopping, noting differences in prices among various brands and sizes of food items.

- Discuss with your students how the trip went, problems (if any) they encountered, and plans for going to the market next time.

Sample Lesson Plan Suggestions for Level IV Students

Content Objective: Shopping at the Market for Food

- Discuss with students what they may need or want help with in food shopping.

- Make sure that they have sufficient knowledge of comparison shopping, budgeting, coupon usage, and nutrition (see Level III). Include a shopping trip and debriefing.

- Identify and discuss newspaper articles from food sections or from various texts on nutrition, cooking, or meal customs from around the world.

- Ask your students to write out favorite recipes, including proportion of ingredients, for self-reference and possible sharing with others. Discuss as a possible project the idea of developing a collaborative cookbook that would have cultural information as well as recipes.

- Have your students identify and share names and locations of various specialty grocery stores or markets in the area.

- Have your students write inquiry or complaint letters or make phone calls to store owners.

- Have your students prepare nutritional information for their children or their families or friends.

SUMMARY

By having your teaching and assessment materials as well as tentative lesson plans ready and available, perhaps in a canvas bag or an attaché case, you'll feel confident and ready for almost any situation that may arise. Relax and remember that you'll not only be affecting other lives but that your own life will never be quite the same. Good luck!

♦ **OPENING A NEW WORLD**

EPILOGUE:
OPENING A NEW WORLD

It will be exciting to watch your students grow as they develop new skills in English. A whole new world will be opened to you as you learn more about your students' countries and cultures and you develop confidence in your ability to teach English to Speakers of Other Languages. Both you and your students will be enriched.

We sometimes forget that most of us are immigrants or descendants of immigrants. What better way to pay homage to our own immigrant ancestors than to reach out a helping hand to the newcomers who have come to live in or visit our land? When we open channels of communication with people of different cultures, our own insights are sharpened, and we can truly conceive of the peoples of the world as brothers and sisters.

We don't choose our native language and customs. We inherit them. But we can share them with others, and we can learn about our students' languages and customs, too. Both students and tutors have something to give and something to gain. The tutors give new skills in English and friendship. The students give us the gift of insight into another culture. May the exchange prove worth the effort to both. Everyone smiles in the same language. So let's smile as we work and learn together as tutors and students.

APPENDIXES

◆ APPENDIXES

APPENDIXES

- ◆ **A - TUTOR-READINESS EVALUATION**

- ◆ **B - GLOSSARY OF TERMS USED IN THE FIELD OF ESOL**

- ◆ **C - THE COMPETENCY-BASED MAINSTREAM ENGLISH LANGUAGE TRAINING (MELT)**

- ◆ **D - SEQUENCE OF SKILLS - A CHECKLIST**

- ◆ **E - CITIZENSHIP INFORMATION**

- ◆ **F - GUIDELINES FOR SELECTING ESOL TEXTBOOKS**

- ◆ **G - MANUSCRIPT/ CURSIVE ALPHABET**

- ◆ **H - CONVERSATION STARTERS**

- ◆ **I - SAMPLE LVA STUDENT INTAKE FORM**

- ◆ **J - COMMENT SHEET**

APPENDIX A

TUTOR-READINESS EVALUATION - LITERACY VOLUNTEERS OF AMERICA, INC.

Attitudes

Before you begin to instruct your students, you should evaluate your attitudes as well as the skills you will need to provide successful instruction in teaching English to Speakers of Other Languages.

1. Am I free of critical attitudes toward those who cannot speak, understand, read, and write English? My answer requires absolute honesty in examining my own attitudes toward people from other countries.

2. Am I willing to be patient with small gains and with the possibility of a long period of instruction?

3. Am I enthusiastic enough in my instruction to provide genuine encouragement so that my students can experience feelings of accomplishment, no matter how minor the success?

4. Am I genuinely interested in learning about different cultures, traditions, and languages?

General Information

1. Am I willing to get more information about my students' countries and cultures?

2. If my students want to become citizens, where will I go for useful information?

Assessment of Students

1. When will I test my students?

2. How will I find out at what level a prospective student

    a. can *understand* English?

    b. can *speak* English?

    c. can *read/write* in his/her native language?

    d. can *read/write* in English?

3. Describe student portfolios and tell how they are important in student assessment.

Teaching Strategies

1. What are the basic attributes in teaching English using the Communicative Approach?

2. What are the four language skills to be included in each lesson?

3. How can you determine what real-life materials and vocabulary your students need and want?

4. What is a suggested sequence of teaching language according to the sequential/balanced formula?

5. What are some practical ways to teach listening and comprehension skills? What gestures can you use?

6. Describe at least three survival skills which can be taught.

7. Give an example of each of the following techniques:
    a. Substitution drill (simple and complex)
    b. Response drill
    c. Transformation drill (negative/positive; statement/question)
    d. Backward buildup
    e. Two creative exercises

8. Write a simple dialogue to be memorized. Describe the steps necessary to teach this dialogue.

9. Describe two ways to help students expand their vocabulary.

10. Describe Language Experience and give an example of how you would use this with ESOL students.

Lesson Planning

1. List several elements that should be included in each lesson plan.

2. When is the best time to make a lesson plan for the next lesson?

Case Histories

In the following case histories, the results of assessment using the ESLOA are given. In practice, such assessment may be your responsibility. If so, testing should be done as soon as possible after the students have been assigned to you. With the following five student case histories, describe what your early lesson plans would include. How would you answer these questions?

1. From what you know about this individual, what specific materials and texts would you use?

2. What techniques, exercises, and activities would you use?

3. What are some other ways you could help this student?

1. **Francisco** is a 19-year-old Sicilian man who has had six years of schooling in Italy. He has been in the United States for one year and lives with his elderly father in an apartment house where Francisco is a maintenance worker. He also works two hours a day as a bagger in a supermarket. His ambition is to join the Air Force where he can fulfill his lifelong ambition of flying planes, but he knows that he must know more English than the few phrases he now speaks.

Francisco's working schedule is such that it is impossible for him to attend adult education classes. He tries to help himself by listening to radio newscasts, but his limited knowledge of English hinders his understanding of their content. He enjoys biking and playing bocce ball. He tests at Level I in *ESLOA*.

2. **Muy** is a Vietnamese woman, 30 years old, who has been in the United States for three months. She has a five-year-old daughter, a six-year-old son, and is expecting another child in six months. Muy speaks fluent French and reads and writes in Vietnamese as well as in French. Her English is halting and difficult to understand because of pronunciation difficulties and a sparse vocabulary. She faces two problems with communication: her inability to converse with her children's teachers and her need to discuss her pregnancy with an English-speaking doctor. She tests at Level II in ESLOA.

3. **Danno** is an 18-year-old boy from Puerto Vallarta, Mexico. He has lived in the United States about eleven months and is in his first year of high school. Because of his language difficulty (he speaks only "street" English and not much of that), he is in danger of dropping out of school. He wants to stay in school because he dreams of being on the track team, but he's falling behind in all of his subjects except math.

His American-born schoolmates harass him because of his school performance and also because he is Mexican. Consequently he has become shy and somewhat surly. He has no special hobbies and spends his time on the streets with older Mexican friends. He tests at Level III in *ESLOA*.

4. **Rosa** is a widow born 53 years ago in a small village in Italy and has recently been brought to the United States by her eldest son. Rosa is unable to read and write in her native language and had no schooling in her little village. She is unhappy because she can converse only with her son since his American wife and children know only a few words of Italian.

Rosa feels like a displaced person; she misses the community life of the village, her neighbors, and her important position as the local midwife. She does not understand the customs and lifestyle of her American family, and her son is often too busy to answer her questions. Crocheting and Sunday mass (which she cannot understand because it is in English) are her only pleasures. She wants to speak and be understood, ask questions, and understand the answers. Reading and writing are unimportant to her right now. She tests at Level I in *ESLOA*.

5. **Bernard** is a 24-year-old Russian Jew who came to this country from the outskirts of St. Petersburg three months ago. He completed high school in Russia, speaks and reads Russian and Hebrew, and has a reading knowledge of English. He is attending adult education classes but needs special tutoring if he is to attain his goal—to be accepted at the university within a year. His English is stilted and hesitant. He usually asks people to slow down when speaking to him, and he's confused by local idioms. He tends to think in Russian and translate into English. He tests at Level IV in ESLOA.

SUMMARY

If you have thought deeply about your attitudes about working with people of other countries and have reviewed the skills you learned through your training and reading this book, know that you can reach out to help your first students. If you have some reservations about how you will handle unknown situations, you are not alone. Be aware, too, that your new students will come to you wondering how this new teaching/learning situation will go. Take *I Speak English* with you to class as your "security blanket," keeping in mind that it provides lots of helpful information. You can be sure that on your own you will find many creative ways to handle special situations.

APPENDIX B

GLOSSARY OF TERMS USED IN THE FIELD OF ESOL

ABE (Adult Basic Education)

ACE (Adult Continuing Education)

ACTFL (American Council on the Teaching of Foreign Languages)

ALM (Audiolingual Method): A behaviorist approach to teaching languages which relies heavily on oral repetition and drills

BICS (Basic Interpersonal Communication Skills): Social language

Bilingual: Proficient in two languages

CALP (Cognitive Academic Language Proficiency): Academic language

CELT (Comprehensive English Language Test)

CLD (Culturally and Linguistically Diverse)

Conversational English: Listening comprehension and speaking skills in English

EFL: English as a Foreign Language

ESL: English as a Second Language

ESOL: English for (or to) Speakers of Other Languages

ESP: English for Specific Purposes

ESLOA (English as a Second Language Oral Assessment): An assessment of oral skills used by LVA, written by Joye Coy Shaffer and Teresa McLean

Functional Illiterate: Any person who cannot read or write well enough in a language to meet daily needs

GED (General Education Development): The equivalent of a high school diploma; can be earned by passing specific proficiency examinations or by fulfilling certain other requirements

Grammar Translation: A method of teaching languages by learning grammar rules and translating into and from any native language

Illiterate: Any person who cannot read or write

L1: The first language, or home language

L2: The second or additional language

LEP (Limited English Proficiency)

Linguistics: A science which systematically analyzes and describes a language as used by its native speakers

Monolingual: Proficient in only one language

Natural Approach: The learning of a foreign language intuitively by using it in natural or real situations

NFE (Nonformal Education)

Primary Language: The language usually learned as a child, generally used for communication

Secondary Language: The language learned as a second language. It can be the language that is used for daily communication.

TEFL (Teaching English as a Foreign Language)

TESL (Teaching English as a Second Language)

TESOL (Teachers [or Teaching] of English to Speakers of Other Languages): The professional organization of ESOL teachers (TESOL, 1600 Cameron Street, Suite 300, Alexandria, VA 22314)

TOEFL (Test of English as a Foreign Language): A standardized test of English as a foreign language. A score of between 500 and 600 is needed for foreign students wishing to enter most American colleges and universities. (Test applications are available from the Educational Testing Service, P.O. Box 899, Princeton, NJ 08541-0008.)

APPENDIX C

THE COMPETENCY-BASED MAIN-STREAM ENGLISH LANGUAGE TRAINING (MELT)

(from the Office of Refugee Resettlement, U.S. Department of Health and Human Services, 330 C Street, SW, Switzer Building, Washington, D.C. 20201)

Part I - Competencies Listed by Topic From Lowest to Highest Levels of Difficulty

> ( ) - Language example for competency statement.
>
> [ ] - Language example that students are expected to listen to and understand.
>
> (" ") - Language example that students are expected to produce.
>
> (CAPITALS) - Language example that students are expected to read and understand.

BANKING

Endorse a check.

Provide proper ID upon request to cash a check or money order. ("Can I cash this check?")

Buy a money order ("A money order for $50.00, please.")

Write a check.

Fill out a money order, including date, amount, name of addressee, own name, and signature.

Fill out deposit/withdrawal slips.

Buy and fill out an international money order.

Fill out the required forms to open a checking or savings account with assistance.

Read a savings and checking account statement.

Fill out a loan application with assistance.

COMMUNITY SERVICES

Read emergency words. (FIRE, POLICE, POISON)

Read, say, and dial telephone numbers of emergency services. (FIRE 991)

Spell name and address and report an emergency in the home by telephone in simple terms. ("Help!" "Police!")

Ask for stamps at a post office. ("Two airmail stamps, please.")

Identify basic facilities, services, and commonly seen community workers in the neighborhood/community. ("bank," "money," "teller," "hospital," "doctor")

Report an emergency in person. ("Help! Fire in Apartment 2A!")

Correctly address an envelope/package, including return address.

Provide upon request proof of address or other necessary information in order to obtain a library card. [Can I see your driver's license?] ("Yes, here you are.")

Report location and problem in an emergency outside the home. ("Help! There's a robbery at 10 Main Street!")

Ask and answer questions about the name of own or child's school, teacher, class, and time. [Which school does your child go to?] ("Lincoln School.")

Read and interpret common signs regarding hours in public areas. (PARK CLOSED AT 6:00)

Fill out a change of address form, with assistance.

Ask simple questions to determine correct postage. ("How much is this letter by airmail?")

Write a note or call to explain an absence from school. ("I was absent yesterday because I went to the dentist.")

Respond to postal clerk's questions regarding customs forms and insurance forms for domestic and overseas packages. [What's inside?] ("Clothing.") [What's the value?] ("$25.00.")

Respond to serious weather conditions based on a TV, radio, or telephone warning. [There's a tornado watch until 10:00 tonight.]

Inquire about the availability of vocational training or adult basic education programs. ("Is there a welding class that I can take?")

Read and respond appropriately to written communications from child's school: shortened school day, vacation, parent-teacher meeting.

Read basic information on child's report card. (P = PASS, F = FAIL)

Ask for information about, and locate on a map, public recreational facilities and entertainment. ("Where can I go fishing?")

Fill out postal forms, such as letter registration forms, without assistance.

Arrange day care or pre-school for own children ("I'd like to enroll my daughter in preschool.")

Assist others in reporting an emergency with limited translation as necessary.

Obtain information about local public recreational facilities and entertainment from prerecorded messages.

Ask about service provided by a public library. ("Can I renew these books?" "Can I borrow records?")

Read information about education, health, and other community services in a community newsletter.

Accompany and assist a person at a clinic or in an emergency room.

Report a suspected loss or theft. ("I didn't get my check in the mail; I think someone stole it.")

Get information from local media sources—newspaper, TV, and radio—on education, legal, health, and other community services.

Obtain a fishing license, legal advice, etc., and order merchandise by mail.

Report problems about mail-order merchandise by telephone or letter. ("I haven't received my order yet. It's two weeks late.")

EMPLOYMENT—FINDING A JOB

State previous occupation in simple terms. ("Cook.")

State current job status. [Do you have a job?] ("No." or "Yes.")

State desire to work in simple terms. ("I want a job.")

State own job skills in simple terms. ("I can cook.")

Copy basic personal information on a simple job application form. (NAME, SOCIAL SECURITY NUMBER, AGE, ADDRESS)

Read HELP WANTED sign.

Identify some common entry-level jobs which can be held by those with limited English ability.

Respond to specific questions about previous work experience using short phrases, including occupation(s), length, and dates of employment. [What was your job?] ("Cook.") [How long?] ("Ten years.")

Fill out a simple job application form, including previous or current position(s) and dates of employment.

Ask others to help in finding a job, e.g., from a sponsor, job developer, or friends. ("I need a job.")

Inquire about job openings and determine a time for an interview in person. ("I …

Sta

A

Exp
  j
  c

Read
  n

Desc
  jo

ing, including degrees of ability. ("I can fix trucks." "I have a lot of experience.")

Read signs and notices posted at work site, agency, etc., advertising positions available; ask for clarification (if necessary).

Indicate several general types of entry-level positions in the U.S. and their respective duties, qualifications, and working hours. ("factory work," "sort parts," "no experience required," "full-time")

Answer basic questions about educational background, including dates and location(s) (by country). [What is your educational background?] ("I finished high school in Iraq in 1970.")

State long-term goals. ("I'd like to be a supervisor.")

Fill out a standard job application form; ask for assistance when needed.

Begin and end an interview appropriately; answer and ask questions and volunteer information, if appropriate.

Find out about benefits for a new job. ("What kinds of benefits are available?")

State own ability related to work. ("I learn quickly.")

Respond appropriately to an employer's decision about a job, whether accepted or rejected. [I'm sorry but the job is filled.] ("Do you have any other openings?")

Make a follow-up call about a job application. ("Did the manager review my application?")

Use a telephone to inquire about advertised and unadvertised job openings for an interview. ("Do you have any job openings?" [Yes, we do.] ("What jobs are available?") Discuss job advancement opportunities, requirements, and procedures with supervisor or counselor. ("I'd like to apply for the position of supervisor. What are the procedures?")

Write a basic resume with assistance.

Write a cover letter and follow-up letter when applying for a job, with assistance.

EMPLOYMENT—ON THE JOB

Ask if a job was done correctly. ("Is this OK?")

Ask simple clarification questions about routine job tasks and instructions. ("Please repeat." "Do this?")

Respond to simple direct questions about work progress and completion of tasks. [Are you finished?] ("No." or "Not yet.")

Ask supervisor or coworker for help. ("Can you help me?")

Sign name on time sheet.

Respond to simple oral warnings or basic commands about safety. [Watch out!]

Read common warning or safety signs at the work site. (DANGER)

Read alpha-numeric codes. (AF 47)

Give simple excuses for lateness or absence in person. ("I was sick yesterday.")

State need for frequently used materials. ("I need boxes.")

Report work progress and completion of tasks. ("I'm finished.")

Find out about file location of common materials and facilities at the work site. ("Where is the supply room?")

Follow simple one-step oral instructions to begin and to perform a task which is demonstrated, including simple classroom instructions. [Put these away.]

Ask for permission to leave work early or to be excused from work. ("Can I go home?")

Give simple excuses for lateness or absence on the telephone. ("My name's Tran. I'm sick today.")

Follow simple oral instructions which contain references to places or objects in the immediate work area. [Get me the box over there.]

Modify a task based on changes in instructions. [Wait! Don't use that!]

Ask/tell where a coworker is. [Where's Tran?] ("He's in the cafeteria.")

Give simple one-step instructions to coworkers. ("Put the tools over there.")

Follow simple two-step directions on the job. [Take this and put it on the shelf.]

Respond to supervisor's comments about quality of work on the job, including mistakes, working too slowly, and incomplete work. ("I'm sorry. I won't do it again.") Give specific reasons for sickness, absence, or lateness. ("I had the flu. I had to go to the doctor.")

Report specific problems encountered in completing a task. ("I don't have any more paper.")

Read first name and department on employer name tags. (ROSE/DEPARTMENT 10)

Respond to multiple-step oral instructions without visual references. [Take the box in the hall to the mailroom and put it on the top shelf.]

Briefly explain a technique or the operation of a piece of basic equipment to a coworker. May use gestures or demonstrate. ("You have to loosen the screw and raise it up.")

State intention to resign and give reasons for resigning from the job. ("I'm going to quit my job in three weeks because I'm moving.")

Request a letter of reference. ("Could you write a reference letter for me?")

Report and describe the nature of problems on the job. ("The stairs are dangerous because they're wet.")

Read a simple work memo, asking for assistance if necessary.

Fill out accident report forms with assistance. Teach a routine task to a coworker using step-by-step verbal instructions and demonstrations.

Read own employment reviews, including explanations of promotion or probation.

Read most simplified on-the-job audio-visual training materials for entry-level jobs.

Read and fill out health insurance forms with the use of bilingual reference materials.

Read basic nontechnical personnel policies and benefit documents with assistance.

Ask about regular paycheck deductions and question irregularities. ("Why is my FICA deduction more this month?")

Read written safety regulations and operating instructions for tools and equipment.

Explain a technique or the operation of a complicated machine such as a drill press.

Initiate and maintain conversations at the work site, such as the advantages or disadvantages of joining a union.

Write a short work memo.

HEALTH

State own general condition in simple terms. ("I'm tired.")

State need for medical help. ("Can you help me? I'm sick.")

Read simple signs related to health care. (HOSPITAL, EMERGENCY, PHARMACY, DRUG STORE)

Identify major body parts. ("Arm," "stomach," "leg")

State major illnesses or injuries. ("Sore throat," "broken arm")

Make a doctor's appointment in person, giving own name, address, and telephone number when asked.

Read time and date for a medical appointment from an appointment card. (THURSDAY, DECEMBER 26, AT 3:00)

State a need for an interpreter. ("I don't speak English. I speak Vietnamese.")

Follow simple instructions during a medical exam. [Open your mouth. Take off your shirt. Take a deep breath.]

Ask for a familiar nonprescription medication at the drug store. ("I want a bottle of aspirin.")

State others' health problems in simple terms. ("His arm hurts.")

Determine and report body temperature as indicated by a thermometer. ("My temperature is 100.")

Ask for a patient's room number. ("What is Sarem Nouan's room number?")

Identify oneself, one's appointment, and doctor's name, if applicable, upon arrival at the doctor's office. ("I'm Sarem Nouan. I have a 2:00 appointment.") [Which doctor?] ("Dr. Smith.")

Ask about and follow simple instructions for using medicine. ("How much?" "How many?")

State symptoms associated with common illnesses. ("I have diarrhea.")

Read the generic names of common nonprescription medicines. (AS-PIRIN, COUGH SYRUP)

Read and follow directions on medicine labels, including abbreviations. (TAKE 2 TSP. 3 TIMES A DAY.)

Ask for assistance in locating common nonprescription medicines. ("Where is the aspirin?")

Follow simple oral instructions about treatment. [Stay in bed. Take one pill every day.]

Locate facilities within a hospital by reading signs. (X-RAY, CAFETE-RIA)

Ask a doctor or nurse about own physical condition or treatment plan using simple language. ("What's the problem/matter?" "Can I go to work?")

Describe own emotional state and explain the reason for it. ("I am sad because I think about my family in Cambodia.")

Make a doctor's appointment on the telephone, giving, name, address, telephone number, and the nature of the problem, and request convenient day and time.

Change or cancel a doctor's appointment in person. ("I'd like to cancel my appointment on March 10.")

Report lateness for a medical appointment by telephone. ("I'm going to be 30 minutes late. Is that OK?")

State results of a visit to a doctor/clinic/hospital to employer or teacher. ("The doctor says I can come back to work.")

Fill out a simple insurance form with assistance.

Respond to simple questions about physical disability. [Do you have any health problems?] ("I have allergies.")

Telephone or write a simple note to school/work explaining own or child's absence due to illness. ("My daughter was absent yesterday because she had the flu.")

Read warnings, storage directions, and emergency instructions. (REFRIGERATE AFTER OPENING, KEEP OUT OF REACH OF CHILDREN)

Describe general medical history orally, including names of major illnesses. ("I had hepatitis in 1980.")

Respond to questions about means of payment. [Do you have Med-icaid or personal insurance?] ("Medicaid.")

Fill out a simple medical history form with assistance. May use bilingual materials, if needed.

Explain own and others' health problems in detail. ("My back hurts when I lift heavy objects.")

Offer advice for health problems. ("You've been sick for a long time. Why don't you see a doctor?")

Fill out a standard medical history form with assistance.

Read about and describe some possible side effects of medication. (DROWSINESS MAY RESULT.)

Read routine clinic notice/reminders —hours, payment requirements, policies concerning canceled appointments.

Read immunization requirements for school and work.

HOUSING

Identify common household furniture/ rooms. ("Kitchen, bathroom.")

Read exit route signs in housing. (EXIT, FIRE ESCAPE)

Identify basic types of available housing. ("Apartment." "House.")

Report basic household problems and request repairs in simple terms. ("The toilet is leaking. Please fix it.")

Report basic household emergencies by telephone—fire, break-ins, etc.; say and spell name, address, and give telephone number when asked.

Answer simple questions about basic housing needs. [What kind of an apartment are you looking for?] ("I need three bedrooms.")

Ask how much the rent is. ("How much is the rent?")

Read common housing signs. (FOR RENT, STAIRS)

Ask for information about housing including location, number of and type of rooms, rent, deposit, and utilities. ("Where is the apartment?" "How many rooms are there?" "How much is the rent?")

Identify total amount due on monthly bills. (AMOUNT DUE: $35.87)

Arrange a time with the landlord or superintendent to make household repairs. ("Can you fix the furnace in the morning?")

Describe own housing situation, including cost, size, and number of household members. ("My apartment is too small.")

Make simple arrangements in person to view housing. ("Can I see the apartment this afternoon?")

State housing needs and ask specific questions in person about cost, size, accessibility to transportation and community services, and basic conditions for rental—date available, number of persons allowed. ("When is the apartment available?" "Where is the nearest bus stop?")

Make arrangements with the landlord to move in or out of housing, including return of deposit. ("I'd like to move in on June 19.")

Question errors of household bills in person. ("There's a mistake on my telephone bill. I didn't make these long-distance calls.")

Ask about and follow special instructions for using/maintaining common household equipment and facilities—defrosting the refrigerator, lighting the pilot, using laundry facilities. ("How do I turn on the heat?")

Ask about and follow special instructions on the use of an apartment or housing. [Take out the garbage on Thursdays.]

Ask to borrow basic tools and household items from a neighbor. ("Excuse me, can I borrow a hammer?")

Arrange for installation or termination of household utilities. ("I'd like to have a telephone installed as soon as possible.")

Question errors on household bills on the telephone. ("I have one phone. Why am I charged for two phones?")

Explain the exact nature or cause of a household problem. ("The bathroom sink is leaking. There's water all over the floor.")

Read classified ads and housing notices.

Read utility meters and bills.

Make complaints to and respond appropriately to complaints from neighbors or the landlord. ("Your dog barks too much. We can't sleep. Can you keep him quiet?")

Ask about and describe landlord/tenant responsibilities. ("The landlord has to pay for the gas.")

State needs and ask specific questions about housing or a rental agreement by telephone. ("Is the rental agreement for one year or for two years?")

Answer questions regarding a lease or rental agreements.

Read a nonsimplified housing lease or rental agreement and fill it out with assistance.

SHOPPING

State basic food needs. ("I need rice.")

Ask the price of food, clothing, or other items in a store. ("How much is this coat?")

Read a limited number of basic store signs. (IN, OUT, SALE)

State basic clothing needs. ("I need a coat.")

Read aisle numbers. (2B)

Differentiate sizes by reading tags. (S, M, or L; 8, 10 or 12.)

Read abbreviations for common weights and measures in a supermarket. (LB., QT.)

Read common store signs. (IN, OUT, UP, DOWN, CASHIER)

Ask about and read signs for store hours. (OPEN, CLOSED; SAT. 9 A.M.-12 P.M.)

Read expiration dates (EXP 4/4/84, SELL BY 4/8/82)

Request size and color for a specific item in simple terms. ("Do you have a small size?")

Ask for information about places to buy food/clothing/household items. ("Where can I buy rice?")

Ask for and follow simple directions to locate food/clothing in a store ("Where are the coats?") [In Aisle 4A.]

Ask for food using common weights and measures. ("One pound of hamburger, please.")

Order and pay for food at a fast-food restaurant. ("A hamburger and a coke, please.")

Read prices and weights of various food items and determine the best buy by comparing. ($1.89/LB., $1.99/LB.)

Respond to cashier's questions concerning means of payment. [Cash or charge?] ("Cash.")

Request a different size or price. ("Do you have a bigger one?")

Ask for a receipt. ("Can I have a receipt, please?")

Express a need to return/exchange merchandise and state satisfaction/dissatisfaction with an item in terms of color, size, fit, etc. ("This is too big.")

Read supermarket/department store newspaper ads or use coupons for comparative shopping. (FLORIDA ORANGES, 5-LB. BAG, $1.79)

Locate items in a supermarket/store by reading common section/department signs. (PRODUCE, HOUSEWARES)

Read a variety of store signs indicating sales or special prices. (REDUCED, TODAY ONLY)

Request a particular color or style of clothing. ("Do you have this in light blue?")

Ask about and follow oral instructions for care of clothing or read labels on clothing in symbols and words. [Wash in cold water.] ("Can I put this in the dryer?")

Read names of different types of stores. (HARDWARE, JEWELRY)

Ask about and understand basic information over the telephone about store hours, products, and prices. ("Do you make keys?")

Read food labels and follow directions for preparing food.

Write a letter to question a bill.

Read consumer protection laws and product warranties.

TRANSPORTATION

Ask the amount of local bus or train fares. ("How much is a bus ticket?")

Read a limited number of symbols or transportation/pedestrian signs. (BUS STOP, WALK/DON'T WALK)

Ask for a transfer. ("A transfer, please.")

Ask for a bus, train, or plane destination. ("Where does this bus go?")

Read signs indicating bus/train destinations and street names. (MAIN STREET)

Ask for information about a location in an airport, bus, or train station. ("Where is Gate 10?")

Respond to and ask basic questions about one's own or others' departure/arrival times. ("When are you leaving?")

Respond to common requests. [Please move to the back of the bus.]

Ask when and where to get off or on a local bus/train. ("I'm going to the post office. Where do I get off?")

Buy bus, train, or plane tickets. ("I'd like a one-way ticket to Chicago.")

Read common signs in an airport or bus/train station. (TO GATES 6-14, TICKETS)

Read common traffic and pedestrian signs. (ONE WAY, KEEP RIGHT, NO PARKING)

Ask where a bus/train is going, where it stops, and which buses/trains stop at a given stop. ("Which bus stops at Main Street and Second Avenue?")

Read an arrival/departure information board in an airport or bus/train station.

Read printed bus/train schedules.

Fill out a state driver's license application.

Ask for information in order to purchase a used car. ("What's the mileage?")

Answer a police officer's questions regarding a car accident or traffic violation. [How fast were you going?] ("55.")

Fill out a car accident report.

Describe common car problems in need of repair. ("My car won't start.")

Ask and answer questions and read information related to buying car insurance.

Get detailed long-distance travel information over the telephone such as schedules and costs. ("What's the cheapest way I can fly round-trip from New York to San Francisco?")

Part II—Additional Competencies Listed by Area. Competencies listed from lowest to highest level of difficulty

CLARIFICATION

Express a lack of understanding. ("I don't understand.")

Ask someone to repeat. ("Please repeat it again.")

Ask someone to speak slowly. ("Please speak slowly.")

Repeat something when asked to do so. ("My name is Tran.") [Could you repeat that?] ("My name is Tran.")

Ask the English word for something. ("What's this?")

Ask the meaning of something written in English. ("What's this?")

Verify the name of something by asking simple yes/no questions. ("Is this the post office?")

Ask for information or clarification using basic question words. ("How?" "Go where?")

Give clarification in response to basic question words. ("Tung is not here.") [Who?] ("Tung.")

Ask someone to spell or write something. ("Can you write it for me?")

Ask about the meaning or the pronunciation of a word. ("What does _____ mean?" "How do you say _____?")

Ask for clarification using a partial question with appropriate gestures. [Go to the cafeteria.] ("Go to _____?")

Spell or write something for purposes of clarification. Repeat instructions to verify comprehension. [Go to Room 4.] ("Room 4?")

Identify which part of instructions or an explanation are not understood. ("I don't understand what to do after I put these away.")

Ask for clarification by giving alternatives. ("Fifteen or fifty?")

Rephrase one's own explanation/ statement. ("He's not here.") [What?] ("He's absent.")

Respond to a listener's need for clarification of own speech by rephrasing. ("Take the box in the hall to the office.") [What?] ("There is a box in the hall. Take it to the office.") Paraphrase complex ideas or difficult concepts.

DIRECTIONS

Ask for the location of common places within a building. ("Where is the bathroom?")

Ask for the location of a place. ("Where is the bus stop?")

Read, say, and copy numbers as used on streets and buildings.

Follow simple oral directions to a place. [Turn right/left. Go straight.]

Respond to simple questions about a destination. [Where are you going?] ("To the bank.")

Follow a simple hand-drawn map to locate a place in an already familiar setting when directions are also given orally. [Go one block. Turn left.]

State the location of own residence by giving the address and nearest streets, or by referring to familiar landmarks. ("I live near the hospital.")

Follow simple oral directions to places in a building. [Upstairs, third floor, to Room 14A]

Give simple directions to a place. ("Turn right/left. Go to the third house.")

Identify own home and major streets or landmarks on a simplified map. ("I live on 22nd Street.")

Find a place by following simple written directions. (GO TWO BLOCKS. TURN LEFT.)

Follow and give multiple-step directions to specific places within a building. ("Go to the second floor and turn right. It's the third door on the left.")

Use a map to find a place.

Give specific instructions in person to a place which is marked clearly on a map. ("Go north three blocks. Turn right on 10th Street. The post office is on the left.")

Write and follow simple directions to a place given over the telephone.

MONEY

Identify United States coins and bills by name and value. ("Dime." "10 cents.")

Read prices on tags or signs. ($1.25)

Use money correctly to pay the total amount requested orally or in written form at a store, post office, vending machine, etc. [That's $9.80.]

Make or respond to a request for change. ("Do you have change?")

Make or respond to a request for specific coins. ("Do you have a dime?")

Read names of coins on coin-operated machine. (NICKELS, DIMES, QUARTERS)

When incorrect change is received, identify and request correct amount of change from a purchase. ("Excuse me, my change should be $5.00.")

Report problems in using coin-operated machines. ("I lost a quarter in the machine.")

Write information related to personal income on forms, such as employment and training applications.

PERSONAL IDENTIFICATION

Respond to basic questions regarding name, ID/Social Security number, country of origin, address, age, birth date, and marital status. [What's your name?] ("Sarem Nouan.")

Indicate which of own names are first, last, and middle. [What's your last name?] ("Tran.")

Spell, read, and print own name.

Copy basic personal information, including name (first and last), ID/Social Security number, address, and age on a simplified form.

Present identification upon request. [Can I see some identification?]

State ability to speak a language other than English. ("I speak Lao.")

State, write, and read basic personal information including names, relationship to, and ages of family members.

Respond to questions about own ethnic group. [Are you Hmong?] ("Yes.")

Spell own name, country of origin, and address when requested.

Respond to questions about own ability to speak, read, and write English and any other language. [Which languages do you know?] ("I can speak Assyrian and Arabic.")

State the number of years of previous education or study of English. [How many years did you go to school?] ("Eight.")

Give the names of familiar people. [Who is your sponsor?] ("Mr. John Doe.")

Fill out a simple form, including name, address, age, signature, country of origin, birthplace, marital status, sex, title (Mr., Mrs., Ms.), citizenship, and maiden name.

State or write own physical characteristics, including height, weight, and color of hair and eyes.

Provide information about a sponsor, including the contact name, agency, address, and telephone number. ("My sponsor is USCC.")

Describe self and members of immediate and extended family, giving details about background.

Fill out a variety of forms, including but not limited to, credit applications, tax forms, medical forms, and school registration forms.

SOCIAL LANGUAGE

Introduce oneself using simple language. ("I'm Sarem.")

Give and respond to simple greetings and farewells. [Hello. How are you?] ("Fine, thanks. And you?")

Excuse oneself politely. ("Excuse me.")

State weather conditions in simple terms. ("It's cold.")

Answer simple questions about personal background and family [How many children do you have?] ("Three.")

State likes and dislikes using simple language. ("I like tea.")

Respond to simple questions about daily activities and weekly routines. [What time do you stop working?] ("5:00.")

State general feelings in simple terms. ("I'm tired." "I'm sad.")

Respond to common gestures such as handshaking, headshaking to indicate yes/no, beckoning, etc.

Initiate and respond appropriately to a variety of greetings and farewells in simple terms. [Have a nice day.] ("Thanks. You, too.")

Introduce family, friends, and co-workers using simple language. ("This is Somay.")

State food and drink preferences in social conversations, using simple language. [Do you want coffee?] ("No; tea, please.")

Respond to simple questions about another person's name and background. [Who's that?] ("Ly.") [Where's she from?] ("Vietnam.")

Ask for assistance in simple terms. ("Can you help me?")

Thank someone for help or for a gift in simple terms. ("Thank you.")

Ask simple questions about daily activities and weekly routines. ("Do you work on Saturdays?")

Make and respond to invitations and offers in person using simple language. [Do you want a ride home?] ("Yes, thank you.")

Ask permission to use or to do something. ("Can I smoke here?")

Give simple compliments about food, clothing, or housing. ("I like your watch.")

Ask simple questions about another person's name and background. ("Who's that?") [Tran] ("Where's he from?") [Vietnam.]

Identify major United States holidays. ("New Year's Day" "Thanksgiving")

Give basic information about the journey from the native country to the United States. ("I went by boat to Indonesia. I stayed in a refugee camp for two years.")

Suggest appropriate clothing/activities based on the weather. ("It's very cold. You should wear a hat.")

Talk about personal interests, recreation, or hobbies. ("I like to cook.")

Ask for information about some common practices on major American holidays in simple terms. ("What do people do on Thanksgiving?")

Thank someone for help or for a gift in a variety of ways. ("Thank you for the gift. It's very nice.")

Respond to and ask questions about personal background, weekend plans, recent experiences, weather, traffic, etc. ("What are you going to do this weekend?" "I'm going to a soccer game.")

Answer questions about differences between the native country and the United States in simple terms. ("In this country, my wife works. I take care of my children.")

Ask about the appropriateness of actions according to the customs/culture in the United States. ("Is it all right to wear my shoes in the house?")

Ask for or offer assistance. ("I'm going to the supermarket. Can I get anything for you?")

Request advice about resolving personal problems. ("I had an accident. What should I do?")

Identify others by description and location rather than by name. ("The woman with the long hair and brown skirt" "The man on the left")

Decline an invitation or postpone a social engagement. ("I'm sorry, I'm busy tomorrow. Can we go shopping next Saturday?")

Initiate and maintain a conversation about movies, TV shows, sports events, and speakers/formal talks on most nontechnical subjects.

Order a meal from a menu in a restaurant.

Respond to and make invitations over the telephone. ("Would you like to go shopping tomorrow?" "Yes, I would.")

Get information about the weather, time, business hours, etc., from most recorded announcements.

Enter into ongoing social conversations on a variety of topics.

TELEPHONE

Note: While use of the telephone in basic survival situations is not expected until later in the teaching, instruction in emergency use of the telephone cannot be postponed until that time.

Identify the symbol or read the sign for a public telephone. (PHONE, TELEPHONE)

Read and be able to dial a limited list of phone numbers such as those for a school, sponsor, or emergency. (911)

Identify oneself on the telephone when answering and calling. ("This is Tran.")

Request to speak to someone on the telephone. ("Tran, please.")

Ask for someone on the telephone. ("Is Tran there?")

Respond to a simple request to "hold" on the telephone. [Please hold.]

When answering the telephone, locate the person requested or indicate that the person is not there, and take the name and telephone number of the caller when necessary. ("Yohanis isn't here.")

Respond appropriately when making or receiving a wrong number call. ("I'm sorry, you have the wrong number.")

Make a long distance call by direct dialing or with the help of an operator.

Take a short telephone message. ("Dr. Smith called. Call him back at 10:00.")

Leave a short message. ("This is Tran. I'll call back at 9:00.")

Use the telephone book to find telephone numbers.

Use the telephone book or call directory assistance to get area codes, long-distance rates, or telephone numbers not listed in the directory.

Respond appropriately to recorded messages and instructions. [At the sound of the tone, leave your name and number.] ("This is Tran. Please call me. My number is _____.")

Use the yellow pages of the telephone book to find specific types of businesses, products, and services.

Make and receive operator-assisted (collect or person-to-person) calls.

Use the telephone to make routine social plans.

Use the telephone to obtain detailed information about products, services, and entertainment.

TIME

Ask and answer basic questions about time, such as days, current months, yesterday/today/tomorrow. [What month is it?] ("February.")

Read clock times on the hour and half hour.

Read and write digital time on the hour, half hour and quarter hour. ("10:15.")

Read the days of the week.

Identify parts of the day—morning, afternoon, evening, and night.

Name and read all the days of the week and the months of the year and their abbreviations.

Read and write dates when expressed in numbers, and read and write months when expressed in words. (5/10/82; MAY 10, 1982)

Read any time expressed in digital terms. (10:23 A.M.)

Ask and answer basic questions about days, months, and years.

Use a calendar.

Ask about and give dates when asked. [When is your daughter's birthday?] ("November 23rd.")

Write the date as requested on a variety of forms.

Ask and answer questions using general time phrases. [When does school start?] ("Next Monday.") [When did you come to the U.S.?] ("Last year.")

Read and write clock times. (A QUARTER AFTER TEN, 10:15, TWENTY MINUTES TO ELEVEN, 10:40)

Literacy Volunteers of America, Inc.

APPENDIX D

SEQUENCE OF SKILLS - A CHECKLIST

Listed below are items that should be taught in sequence. The sequence suggested in any of the areas (structures, time, objects, etc.) is just that: suggested! You may find yourself teaching a structure in the intermediate level before something else because that's what your student needs. That's perfectly all right. You're helping your student meet individual immediate needs. The progression helps give you some order. Use it to your advantage.

Structures[1]

Beginning

Verbs - Simple present (I go. You go. He, she, it goes, etc.)

Verb + "to be" + adjective (I am happy, etc.)

Verb + "to be" + noun (I am a boy.)

Present continuous (I am walking.)

Questions - Information   What (about things)

Where (about places)

When (about time)

Who (about people)

How many/much (about numbers or quantity)

Why/because (about actions)

Yes/No

Simple present (Do you eat lunch at noon? Yes, I do.)

Simple present "to be" (Are you a student? Yes, I am.)

Present progressive (Are you going to the store? No, I'm not.)

Choice questions

Simple present (Do you walk or run? I run.)

Present progressive (Is he running or walking? He's walking.)

Pronouns - Personal (I, you, he, she, it, we, they)

Possessive (mine, yours, his, hers, its, our, their)

Adjectives - Possessive (my, your, his, her, its, our, their)

Demonstrative (this, that, these, those)

Prepositions of place (to, at, in, on, under, behind, near, etc.)

Conjunctions (and, or)

1. *Adapted from* Guide to Learning Better English *by Lee Hickock Lacy (International Student Exchange, Washington, D.C.)*

Intermediate

Verbs -   Simple past (regular: I climbed; irregular: I sang; "to be": I was a fireman.)

Future ("going to" + verb: I am going to sing. "will" + verb: I will run.)

Questions -   Information (see Beginning Level)

Yes/No

Simple past (Did I climb? Yes, I did.)

Future (Am I going to eat? Yes, I am. Will we run? No, we won't.)

Choice questions

Simple past (Did he run or walk? He walked.)

Future (Are we going to New York or San Francisco? We're going to New York.)

Pronouns -   Review personal and possessive from Beginning Level.

Object (me, you, her, him, it, us, them)

Adjectives -   Possessive (see Beginning Level)

Conjunctions (and, but, or)

Advanced

Verbs -   Past continuous (I was sitting.)

Questions -   Information (see Beginning Level)

Yes/No

Past continuous (Was she sitting? Yes, she was.)

Choice questions (Were they sitting or climbing? They were climbing.)

Pronouns-   Review personal and possessive from Beginning Level

Indefinite (somebody, someone, one, no one, nobody, etc.)

Relative (who, which, that)

Conjunctions (because, while, etc.)

Numbers/Prices[2]

1 - 10	10¢ - dime
Telephone numbers	25¢ - quartet
Some street numbers	ordinal numbers (first, second, third, etc.)
11 - 100	50¢ - half dollar
1¢ - penny	$1.00, $2.00, $5.00, etc.
5¢ - nickel	combination of dollars and cents ($2.36)

Time

hour (one o'clock, six o'clock)
before (to) seven) noon, midnight
half hour (1:30, 6:30)

quarter hour (1:15, quarter of four; fifteen
minutes after the hour (twenty past eight; 8:20)
minutes before the hour (ten of (before, to) one)

Months/Days

days of the week (Monday, Tuesday, etc.)

months of the year (January, February, etc.)

dates with numbers (May first or May 1, etc.)

Nouns

(Food, Clothes, Furniture, etc.)

countable nouns (those which can be used with numbers and singular or
plural verbs - i.e. apple, orange, dress, suit, tie, table, chair, mirror, etc.)

uncountable nouns (those which cannot be used with numbers and take a sin
gular verb—i.e., meat, butter, coffee, wool, clothing, darkness, day

2. Adapted from a paper by Lutheran Immigration and Refugee Service, "The Early Days," 1980.

APPENDIX E

CITIZENSHIP INFORMATION

Many conversational English tutors will have students whose ultimate aim is attaining United States or Canadian citizenship. Most cities have citizenship classes either in the public schools or run by community groups, and the student advanced enough to be working for citizenship should be studying in such classes. Your role as an English tutor is important because the ability to understand, speak, read, and write English is a basic requirement for U.S. or Canadian citizenship, with only a few exceptions.

A substantial part of your tutoring session for this type of advanced student should be spent on the material to be covered in the Naturalization Examination. It will be helpful to your student if you have some basic knowledge of the requirements for United States or Canadian citizenship.

U.S. Citizenship Requirements

The applicant seeking U.S. citizenship must

1. have five years legal, permanent residence in the United States

2. be at least 18 years of age

3. be able to speak, read, write, and understand simple English

4. have some knowledge of our form of government and of U.S. history

5. be of good moral character

6. show understanding of, and belief in, the Constitution of the United States

These are the exceptions to the basic requirements:

A foreigner married to a spouse who has lived in the United States for three years, and been a U.S. citizen for at least three years, may have only three years residence in the United States to qualify for citizenship. However, the   requirement to speak, read, and write English still stands.

A person over 50 years of age with 20 years or more of residence in the United States may become a citizen even though he or she cannot speak, read, or write English.

Naturalization Procedures

If the applicant meets the basic requirements, the steps toward citizenship are as follows:

1. Obtain an application (Form N-400) for citizenship, a fingerprint card, and a Biographic Information Form from the nearest office of the Immigration and Naturalization Service, the clerk of a

Naturalization Court, or a social service agency in the community. The application, fingerprint form, and Biographic Information Form must be filled out and mailed to the nearest Immigration and Naturalization Office. (there is an opportunity for the tutor to help the student in this beginning step toward citizenship by explaining the questions in the above forms).

2. After an examination of the application, the applicant will be helped in filing a Petition for Naturalization in the Naturalization Court. There is a $50 fee for filing.

3. After the petition has been filed, the applicant must wait at least 30 days to be notified to appear before the Court for a final hearing. The judge does not ordinarily ask any questions of the applicant because the naturalization examiner has already done so; the latter merely informs the judge that the applicant has been found qualified and should be made a citizen. The applicant then takes an oath of allegiance to the United States.

This brief review of the steps to citizenship can be supplemented by the free pamphlet available from the U.S. Department of Justice, Immigration, and Naturalization Service, entitled "Naturalization Requirements and General Information."

NATURALIZATION EXAMINATION

A big challenge for many people in obtaining citizenship is the Naturalization Examination, which is part literacy (reading and writing English) and the other part history and government of the United States.

Oath of Naturalized Citizens
(from the American Heritage Library)

You will want to explain and simplify much of the information on citizenship. For example, here is the United States oath of naturalized citizens. As you read it, think to yourself how very difficult and confusing the words would be to you if English were not your native language:

"I hereby declare, on oath, that I absolutely and entirely renounce and abjure all allegience and fidelity to any foreign prince, potentate, state, or sovereignty of whom or which I have heretofore been a subject or citizen; that I will support and defend the Constitution and laws of the United States of America against all enemies, foreign and domestic; that I will bear true faith and allegiance to the same; and that I take this obligation freely without any mental reservation or purpose of evasion; so help me God. In acknowledgement whereof I have hereunto affixed my signature."

You might explain its meaning more simply in this manner:

"As a citizen of only the United States, I promise to obey all the laws of this country. I will defend the United States against all its enemies. I will serve in the armed services of the U.S.A. or do noncombatant service, if required. I make this pledge of my own free will, as an oath before God."

Canandian Citizenship Requirements

There are seven requirements for becoming a Canadian citizen.;

1. Legal entry—You must have been lawfully admitted to Canada for permanent residence, i.e. as a landed immigrant.

2. Age—You must be 18 years of age or older to apply for yourself.

3. Residence—You must have lived in Canada for a total time of three years within the four years immediately before your application for citizenship.

   This means that absences from Canada are allowed as long as your time in Canada adds up to three years, but only the four years up to the day you apply for citizenship are considered. Within that time, the period of residence is calculated as follows:

   > one half day for each day in Canada before the date of becoming a landed immigrant, and one day for each day in Canada after the date of becoming a landed immigrant.

4. Freedom from prohibitions—You cannot receive citizenship or take the oath of citizenship (i) if you are considered to be a risk to Canada's security, (ii) if you are under a deportation order, (iii) if you are on probation or parole, (iv) if you are in prison, or (v) if you have been convicted of an indictable offense within the past three years. Time spent in prison or on probation or parole does not count towards a period of residence.

5. Official language—You must know either English or French, the official languages of Canada, well enough to make yourself understood in the community. (Courses in English and French are available from many schools and community organizations.)

6. Knowledge of Canada—You must have some knowledge of your rights and responsibilities as a Canadian citizen and of Canada's political system, geography, and history. Information on these subjects is contained in "The Canadian Citizen" and "A Look at Canada," the free instructional pamphlets which the Citizenship Court will give you.

7. Oath of Citizenship—Finally, you take and sign the Oath of Citizenship:

   > "I swear/affirm that I will be faithful and bear true allegiance to Her Majesty Queen Elizabeth the Second, Queen of Canada, Her Heirs and Successors, according to law and that I will faithfully observe the laws of Canada and fulfill my duties as a Canadian citizen."

   There are Citizenship Courts and Offices in more than 30 cities across Canada. Consult the Government of Canada section of your phone book or write to: Registrar of Canadian Citizenship, Department of the Secretary of State, Ottawa, Ontario K1A 0M5.

APPENDIX F

GUIDELINES FOR SELECTING ESOL TEXTBOOKS

Ask yourself these questions as you look for an appropriate text for your ESOL students.

METHOD

1. Is the approach consistent with your teaching method?
2. Is the approach student centered?
3. Is the approach varied?

SUBJECT MATTER

4. Is the subject matter of current interest?
5. Is cultural and other information up-to-date and accurate?
6. Is the subject matter varied and appropriate to the interests of adult students?

USE

7. Is the text easy to use?
8. Is the text flexible enough to be used in a variety of ways?
9. Is there a teacher's manual or preface which explains how the text can best be used?

FORMAT

10. Does the text provide plenty review of newly introduced material in subsequent lessons?
11. Are exercises and activities usable with one student or a small group, rather than requiring a larger group of students to be effective?
12. Do the exercises require the students to engage in a variety of activities?
13. Are there exercises that allow the students to engage in meaningful communication?

APPEARANCE

14. Are the illustrations lifeless or realistic?
15. Is the print adequate or too small?
16. Is the layout cluttered or easy to look at?

CULTURAL STABILITY

17. Does the text avoid giving the impression that all Americans are white Anglo-Saxon?

18. Does the text avoid racist and sexist stereotypes, and is ethnic stereo-typing avoided?

ILLUSTRATIONS

19. Are there clear illustrations that aim to help students understand new vocabulary and structure?

20. Do the illustrations show individuals of both sexes and different racial and ethnic groups?

BIBLIOGRAPHY

Abdel Messin Daoud and Marianne Celce Murcia, "Selecting and Evaluating a Textbook," in Marianne Celce Murcia and Lois McIntosh, eds., *Teaching English as a Second or Foreign Language* (Rowley, MA: Newbury House, 1979), pp. 302-307.

Mildred R. Donoghue and John F. Kunkle, *Second Languages in Primary Education* (Rowley, MA: Newbury House, 1979), pp, 119-120.

APPENDIX G

D'NEALIAN™ ALPHABET

D'NEALIAN™ MANUSCRIPT ALPHABET

a b c d e f g h i j k l m
n o p q r s t u v w x y z
A B C D E F G H I J K L M
N O P Q R S T U V W X Y Z

D'NEALIAN™ CURSIVE ALPHABET

a b c d e f g h i j k l m
n o p q r s t u v w x y z
A B C D E F G H I
J K L M N O P 2
R S T U V W X Y Z

D'NEALIAN™ NUMBERS

0 1 2 3 4 5 6 7 8 9

APPENDIX H

CONVERSATION STARTERS FOR LEARNING ABOUT INTERNATIONAL STUDENTS

FOOD

1. How many meals a day do people usually eat in your country?
2. What would you eat and drink at each of these meals?
3. Where do you get most of your food?
4. What would you say is the favorite vegetable? meat? fish? dessert?
5. What food would you serve a favorite guest?
6. Is your country famous for a special crop?
7. Please explain how to make one of your favorite meals.

SHELTER

1. Please describe what a typical home looks like in your country.
2. How many rooms does the average apartment or home have?
3. What furniture is inside a typical house in your country?
4. Are any homes air-conditioned or heated?
5. Are the walls painted or is wallpaper used?

CLOTHING

1. What do young children wear to school in your country?
2. What kind of clothes do men and women wear to work?
3. What kind of clothes do men and women wear to a party?
4. Is there special clothing to sleep in?
5. Do fashions change frequently?

TRANSPORTATION

1. Do many people walk to work or school, or do they use bicycles or other forms of transportation?
2. Do many people own automobiles?
3. How much money does a taxicab driver charge in your country? What are the tipping customs?

VALUES IN THE CULTURE

1. Is certain behavior allowed in the home but not in public?
2. How are people punished for disobeying the law?
3. What's considered the most serious crime a person can commit?
4. Do high school students have religious education at school?

5. What is the attitude in your country toward the death penalty?

SCHOOLS

1. Do you have a special preparatory school for university in your country?

2. How many classes a week do high school students have?

3. Is it difficult for high school graduates to find a job?

4. What status do college students have in the society?

5. Are there any differences in the quality of education between a public and a private school?

ATTITUDES TOWARD ANIMALS

1. Do children keep a dog or cat as pets in their home?

2. Would you see an aquarium in some homes?

3. What is done for sick animals?

4. Are there any wild animals in your country?

5. What animals are useful?

SOCIAL STRUCTURE

1. What is the size of an average family?

2. Do grandparents live in the same house?

3. What are the responsibilities of each member of the family?

4. Do married women work?

5. Who takes care of the children?

6. Is it customary for the family to gather around the dinner table and talk?

7. Do the children often fight among themselves?

8. How do people feel about divorce?

9. What is the acceptable way of meeting someone to marry?

10. When does a child leave his home to be on his own?

CHILDREN

1. How do parents decide on a name for their baby?

2. Do children have a certain share in work at home?

3. Do children start school at an early age?

4. Do boys and girls have the same education? Do they go to the same school?

5. Where do children play?

6. Do children have a favorite game they like to play?

7. How are children expected to behave with adults?

8. Are parents strict in disciplining their children?

9. Who punishes children—the mother or father or both?

10. Please tell me a favorite story children know.

11. What songs did you learn at an early age?

SOCIAL GROUPS

1. Do people of different social groups live in different neighborhoods?

2. How is prejudice against minority groups shown in your country?

3. How strong are class distinctions?

4. Do people speak different languages in different parts of your country?

5. Do women often visit local beauty salons?

6. Do children wear uniforms in your schools?

7. What is the most common religion in your country?

8. Do people discuss religion a lot?

LEISURE-TIME ACTIVITIES

1. Do you like American films? Which ones?

2. What type of movies do you like?

3. Who are your favorite actors or actresses?

4. What movies have you seen in your country?

5. What kind of music do you listen to?

6. Do you like American music?

7. Do you have a radio? a record player or tape recorder? a TV?

8. Do most cities have libraries? Are they free?

9. What kind of books do you read?

10. Are there special community centers that provide sports activities?

11. Are there volunteer activities available? What are some common forms of charity?

12. What do university students do in their leisure time?

13. Does the family share activities outside the home? What are these activities?

14. Are there many museums open to the public?

LANGUAGE FORMULAS AND GESTURES

1. How would you introduce me to your family?

2. Would I be expected to shake hands?

3. What would be the polite way for me to leave after a social evening at your home?

4. Would I be expected to bring a gift?

5. What do people say and do after they are introduced?

6. What do you say to another person when you see him in the morning? evening?

HOLIDAYS AND CEREMONIES

1. Is Sunday a legal holiday?

2. What special holidays do you celebrate in your country?

3. How do you celebrate them?

4. Describe a marriage ceremony in your country. Describe a funeral.

COMMUNITY UNITS

1. Do most of the people in your country live in cities, small towns, or farms? Describe them.

2. Are there many factories in the cities?

3. What products are produced?

Reprinted by permission of Dr. V. F. Allen, Temple University, Philadelphia, PA

APPENDIX I

CONFIDENTIAL   DATE_____

LVA LEARNER INTAKE/PERMANENT RECORD

For Local Office Use Only (Please use blue or black ink)   Interviewed by:_____

Type of Program:

- ❏ Regular   ❏ Corrections   ❏ Workplace
- ❏ Family   ❏ Migrant   ❏ In-School
-                            ❏ Other

Program: ❏ BR   ❏ ESL
Instruction: ❏ OTO   ❏ SmGp
Tutor Assigned:_____
Status: ❏ Active   ❏ Transfer/Return
               ❏ No Test   ❏ Terminated
               ❏ No Match

Type of Institution:

- ❏ Library   ❏ Corrections   ❏ Agency
- ❏ School   ❏ Other

Learner Information: Learner ID Code_____

Name_____

Address_____

City/State/Zip_____ Okay to Mail? ❏ Yes ❏ No

Phone (H): ( )_____Okay to Call? ❏ Yes ❏ No

Phone (W): ( ) _____(ext.) OK to Call? ❏ Yes ❏ No

Native Language:_____ ❏ Speak ❏ Read ❏ Write

Date of Birth_____
❏ Male   ❏ Female
Place of Birth_____
U.S. Citizen ❏ Yes ❏ No
Yrs. in U.S._____
Marital Status ❏ M ❏ S ❏ D
Parent ❏ Yes ❏ No
#of Children_____

Ethnic Group:___

1 European-American
2 Afro-American
3 Hispanic-American
4 Native-American
5 Asian-American
6 Mixed American

Education:____

1 Grade 0-4
2 Grade 5-8
3 Grade 9-11
4 H.S. Diploma
5 Some College
6 Not Available

Employment Status:____

1 Full-time
2 Part-time
3 Unemployed
4 Disabled
5 Retired
6 Not in Labor Market
7 Seeking Work
8 Info Not Available

Why dis learner come
to this program?

_____
_____
_____

Source of Referral____

1 TV
2 Radio
3 Friend/Family
4 Employer
5 Library
6 Other Agency
7 Other Literacy Organization
8 Poster
9 Literacy Hotline
10 Other
11 Not Available
12 Special Event
13 PR Talk

Income Level:____

1 (<5,000)
2 (5-9,999)
3 (10-14,999)
4 (15-19,999)
5 (20-24,999)
6 (>25,000)
7 Not Available
8 On Public Assistance

Occupation:____

1 Professional
2 Managerial
3 Clerical
4 Technical
5 Service
6 Agricultural
7 Homemaker
8 Sales
9 Inmate
10 Other

Told of Programs Offered?   ❏ Yes   ❏ No

Referred to Another Agency: ❏ Yes   ❏ No Where? _____

Available to Meet:

Mon	❏ Morn	❏ After	❏ Eve
Tues	❏ Morn	❏ After	❏ Eve
Wed	❏ Morn	❏ After	❏ Eve
Thurs	❏ Morn	❏ After	❏ Eve
Fri	❏ Morn	❏ After	❏ Eve
Sat	❏ Morn	❏ After	❏ Eve
Sun	❏ Morn	❏ After	❏ Eve

Interests_____
_____
_____
_____
_____

Instruction Preference:

❏ OTO   ❏ Small Group   ❏ Either

Tutor Preference:_____

Location Preference:_____

Transportation Mode: _____

Special Needs: ❏ Hearing Impaired

❏ Physically Disabled   ❏ Wheelchair

❏ Teen   ❏ Irregular Meeting Times

Initial Assessment:

❏ ESLOA ❏ READ (Part III) Score:

❏ Other Tests Name:_____

Score:

APPENDIX J

COMMENT SHEET

To *I Speak English* readers from the author, Ruth Colvin:

I hope this book has been helpful as you teach others to understand, speak, read, and write English. I am always looking for more practical and realistic ways to share with others. Your comments and suggestions are always appreciated. Do send them to me at the following address. Thank you.

Ruth Colvin,
Literacy Volunteers of America, Inc.
635 James St.
Syracuse, NY 13203

FAX: 315-472-0002, Email: LVANAT@aol.com

Comments and suggestions about *I Speak English:*

Name:_____

Address:_____

Date:_____

_____
_____
_____
_____
_____
_____
_____
_____
_____
_____
_____
_____
_____

SOURCES CITED

Auerbach, E. (1995). From Deficit to Strength: Changing Perspectives on Family Literacy. In *Immigrant Learners and Their Families*. Gail Weinstein-Shr and Elizabeth Quintero, eds., 63-76. McHenry, IL: Center for Applied Linguistics and Delta Systems Co., Inc.

Auerbach, E. (1992). *Making Meaning Making Change: Participatory Curriculum Development for Adult ESL Literacy*. McHenry, IL: Center for Applied Linguistics and Delta Systems Co., Inc.

Bonham, L. A. (1988). Learning Style Instruments: Let the Buyer Beware. In *Lifelong Learning,* Vol. 11, No. 6, 12-16.

Cheatham, J. C., Colvin, R.J., and Laminack, L. L. (1993). *TUTOR, A Collaborative Approach to Literacy Instruction*. Syracuse, NY: Literacy Volunteers of America, Inc.

CULTURGRAMS: *The Nations Around Us*. 2 Volumes. (1991). Salt Lake City and Provo, Utah: The David M. Kennedy Center for International Studies, Brigham Young University.

Durant, W. (1954). *Our Oriental Heritage*. New York: Simon & Schuster.

Freire, P (1970). *Pedagogy of the Oppressed*. New York: Seabury.

Flavier, J. (1970). *Doctors of the Barrios*. Quezon City, Philippines: New Day.

Gattegno, C. (1963). *The Silent Way: Teaching Foreign Languages in Schools*. New York: Educational Solutions, Inc.

Gramer, M.F. (1994). *The Basic Oxford Picture Dictionary*. New York: Oxford University Press.

Hadley, A. O. (1993). *Teaching Language in Context*. Second edition. Boston: Heinle & Heinle.

Hines, M.E. (1980). *Skits in English*. New York: Regents Publishing Company, Inc.

Hall, E. (1966). *The Hidden Dimension*. Garden City, NY: Doubleday.

McMichael, C. and Coor, M. (1983). *A Guide to Gestures in the ESL Classroom*. Unpublished paper. TESOL, North Texas University in Denton.

Morley, J. (1991a). The Pronunciation Component in Teaching English to Speakers of Other Languages. In *TESOL Quarterly* 25, 481-520.

Morley, J. (1991b). Listening Comprehension in Second/Foreign Language Instruction. In *Teaching English as a Second or Foreign Language*. Second edition. Marianne Celce-Murcia, ed., 81-106. Boston: Heinle & Heinle.

Nash, A., Cason, A., Rhum, M., McGrail, L., and Gomez-Sanford, R. (1992). *Talking Shop: A Curriculum Sourcebook for Participatory Adult ESL*. McHenry, IL: Center for Applied Linguistics and Delta Systems Co., Inc.

Parnwell, E.C. (1988). *The New Oxford Picture Dictionary*. New York: Oxford University Press.

Shaffer, J. C. and McLean, T. (1996). *English as a Second Language Oral Assessment (ESLOA)*. Syracuse, NY: Literacy Volunteers of America, Inc.

Tuckman, B.W. and Jensen, M.A.C. (1977). Stages of Small Group Development Revisited. In *Group and Organizational Studies*, 419-427.

Vella, J. (1994). *Learning to Listen, Learning to Teach*. San Francisco: Jossey-Bass Publisher.

ANNOTATED BIBLIOGRAPHY: FOR ADULT ESOL CLASSES

The following suggestions for further reading were compiled by Elizabeth Holden, Erika Sacks, Joan Shin, and Theresa Sullivan. They are all students in the MA Program in ESOL/Bilingual Education at the University of Maryland, Baltimore County.

ESOL Instructional Resources for Speaking

Dornyei, Z. and Thurrell, S. (1992). *Conversation and Dialogues in Action*. Wilshire, Great Britain: Prentice Hall International.

This book strives to develop conversational skills by focusing on turn-taking, opening and closing conversations, interruptions, and more. Because conversations are interactive, the activities used to develop conversational skills in this text are student-centered.

Genzel, R. B., & Graves C. M. (1994). *Culturally Speaking: A Conversation and Culture Text*. Boston: Heinle & Heinle.

As its title suggests, this book's aim is to have students communicate effectively and appropriately in varying cultural contexts. They will be able to develop insights into North American culture and attitudes by comparing the new culture with their own.

Golebiowska, A. (1993). *Getting Students to Talk*. Wilshire, Great Britain: Prentice Hall International.

Although this book is a supplement to a corresponding course book, it is itself a source book of activities for developing communicative proficiency. It fosters oral competence in combination with non-linguistic tools like gestures, intonation, and distance. In addition, it suggests ways to increase student interest and motivation.

Richards, J. C. with Hull, J. and Procter, S. (1991). *International Communication*. Melbourne, Australia: Cambridge University Press.

This text establishes and extends foundations for communicative competence, according to the situation, purpose, and roles of participants. Higher-level comprehension skills are also developed. A cassette is available for students to use for self-study.

Sion, C., ed. (1991). *More Recipes for Tired Teachers: Well Seasoned Activities for the ESOL Classroom*. New York: Addison-Wesley Publishing Company, Inc.

This book uses simple, student-centered activities to develop communicative skills. The lessons can be easily modified depending on age levels, numbers of students, and the amount of time allotted per lesson.

ESOL Instructional Resources for Pronunciation

Baker, A. and Goldstein, S. (1990). *Pronunciation Pairs*. New York: Cam-bridge University Press.

Pronunciation is practiced through a variety of activities such as dialogues, games, and puzzles. The book is full of illustrations which can be used to spark interest. An audio tape is included

Gilbert, J. (1984). *Clear Speech*. New York: Cambridge University Press.

In this book the chapters are clearly subdivided into word units, thought units, clarity of sounds, listening, and clear speech. A variety of practice exercises are included. The book includes self-analysis to determine trouble spots in pronunciation. The book is accompanied by a cassette tape.

Graham, C. (1988). *Jazz Chants*. New York: Oxford University Press.

This book offers practice of English pronunciation through rhythmic chants. Jazz chants are especially useful in teaching natural rhythmical stress and intonation, using an energetic approach. The book can be used in conjunction with a cassette tape.

Hagen, S.A. and Grogan, P. E. (1992). *Sound Advantage*. Englewood Cliffs, NJ: Regents/Prentice Hall.

This book explores troublesome consonants. Production exercises and pretests to diagnose problem areas are included, as are a wide variety of practice activities and methods for teaching pronunciation.

Morley, J. (1979). *Improving Spoken English: An Intensive Personalized Program in Perception, Pronunciation, Practice in Context*. Ann Arbor: The University of Michigan Press.

This book includes work on stress, rhythm, intonation, and other features of pronunciation. It includes practical activities in listening and speaking to help students gradually improve their speaking and pronunciation skills. It also includes explanations to help students monitor their own pronunciation.

Orion, G. F. (1988). *Pronouncing American English*. New York: Newbury House Publications.

This book concentrates on vowel sounds and consonant sounds each in individual chapters. Emphasis is on the mechanics of speech and how to produce different sounds. It is useful for students at all levels.

ESOL Instructional Resources for Listening

Morley, J. (1976). *Listening Dictation: Understanding English Sentence Structure*. Ann Arbor: The University of Michigan Press.

Practical suggestions to help students understand what they hear by listening, repeating, and finally writing. Teacher dictation scripts are included. Accompanying audio tapes can be used. Listening Dictation is designed to develop discriminative listening and requires active involvement.

Morley, J. (1972). *Improving Aural Comprehension*. Ann Arbor: The University of Michigan Press.

This is a workbook to help students develop disciplined listening. It guides students in what to listen for, when to listen, and how to listen.

ESOL Instructional Resources for Reading

Ediger, A. R. and Srutwa, K. (1989). *Reading for Meaning: Skill Development for Active Reading*. White Plains, NY: Longman.

This book is based on factual reading and literary works. It is geared for the low-intermediate adult learner. Its themes are informative and functional. Passages are designed to stimulate discussion and touch emotions. Follow-up activities include thinking questions, charts, graphs, and pictures. Techniques such as scanning and skimming are taught as well.

Markstein, L. (1994). *Developing Reading Skills: Beginning*. Second edition. Boston: Heinle & Heinle.

This book uses practical topics that students can relate to and apply to their lives such as education, city life, and sports. It is designed for adult learners. Each of the five units is integrated by a common cross-cultural theme and includes a variety of exercises and games.

Newman, C. M., Grognet, A. G., and Crandall, J.A. (1993). *LifePrints: ESL for Adults*. Syracuse, NY: New Readers Press.

This book is designed for beginning adult readers. It deals with practical issues such as getting a job, money choices, driving a car, health, and education. The workbook format provides many activities and opportunities for application of material. A cassette tape is also available.

Pickett, W. P. (1994). *Far From Home: Reading and Word Study.* Second edition. Boston: Heinle & Heinle.

This reading book emphasizes word study. It is useful for advanced beginner to low intermediate level students. The book presumes knowledge of basic structures of English and common words. Activities include story completion and word guessing.

Sosna, B.L. and Abdulaziz, H.T. (1985). *Momentum: Developing Reading Skills.* New York: Harcourt, Brace & Co.

This book is for the beginning adult reader. Issues of common concern are addressed, such as, medicine, energy, food, business, and computers. The first lesson presumes little knowledge of English. Activities include tasks such as identifying the main idea in a passage. Complex issues are introduced gradually.

Woods, E. and Lancaster, B. (1994). *Reading for Survival in Today's Society.* Books 1 & 2. Glenview, IL: Good Year Books.

Readings are practical and related to basic everyday living and necessities for survival. This includes finding a job, keeping a job, making wise purchases, managing money, following directions, finding one's way, purchasing food, living on your own, and dealing with the government. Different styles and formats in which printed ideas appear are explored in a relevant manner.

ESOL Instructional Resources for Writing

Clark, B. L. (1985). *Talking About Writing: A Guide for Tutor and Teacher Conferences.* Ann Arbor: University of Michigan Press.

While this book is designed for use in an academic tutoring context, the author explores both the writing process and the tutoring process. It suggests ways of gen-

erating topics, drafting and reworking ideas, addressing grammar and mechanics, and responding to the learner's writing. Each chapter includes exercises, sample essays, and a selected bibliography. Its conversational tone and its emphasis on the tutoring process make it a worthwhile resource.

Dean, M. (1988). *Write It: Writing Skills for Intermediate Learners of English.* Cambridge: Cambridge University Press.

This text is arranged in units that focus on writing skills. Written for the learner at the intermediate level, it moves the learner toward more academic writing tasks. Each unit has a corresponding audio cassette and begins with a speaking activity that leads to written work. While it is designed for classroom use, it can be adapted for one-to-one tutoring. It is divided into units by length and scope of the writing type, beginning with brief personal writing and moving towards extensive writing about evaluations and opinions. Each unit highlights grammar structures that are useful for each writing function. The teacher's book contains the objective of each unit, the procedure, and a transcript of the audio cassette.

Gati, S. (1992). *Literacy in Lifeskills.* Heinle & Heinle: Boston.

Adult ESOL learners who do not possess literacy skills in their first language or have had limited exposure to the Roman alphabet will benefit from this textbook and the writing activities it provides. It concentrates on the basics of letter formation and handwriting in the context of life skills. Learners are provided with practice in filling out forms, providing personal information, writing numbers and rates, and other skills needed by adults. There are two levels: a textbook for pre-beginners and one for low beginners. Also available are picture cards and a teacher's guide.

Haynes, J. (1995). *American Handwriting Slow and Easy.* McHenry, IL: Delta Publishing Co.

This book offers methods and helpful hints for tutors to use in writing instruction. The book teaches everyday script that is legible to people who use both print and cursive. This book is for adolescents and adults who are unfamiliar with Roman letters or those students who do not know how to write in their native language. Activities include learning to sign your name, fill in blanks and boxes on a form, address an envelope, express dates with numbers, take phone messages, send a package, and fill out applications.

London B. L. and Lee, L. (1994). *The Multi-cultural Workshop: A Reading and Writing Program.* Book 1. Boston: Heinle & Heinle.

This book is designed for adults at a high-beginner or intermediate level. Reading and writing are integrated. It aims to increase vocabulary and critical thinking skills and is appropriate for learners who are considering academic studies.

Marcus, A. (1996). *Writing Inspirations: A Fundex of Individualized Activities for English Language Practice.* Brattleboro, VT: Prolingua Association Publications.

This book is an index of ideas and activities to spark thought, conversation, and written work. Activities reflect real life experiences and range in difficulty from beginner through advanced. This book is especially useful for tutors and adult learners. It can be used by individuals, pairs, or groups. This reference resource book can be photocopied and contains cards which are simple to use.

Newman, C. M., Grognet, A.G,. and Crandall, J.A. (1994). *Lifeprints: ESL for Adults.* New Readers Press: Syracuse, NY.

This textbook takes an integrated, skills approach: it provides a combination of reading, listening, speaking, and writing opportunities. Some of the writing exercises include sentence completion, letter writing, and compiling lists. The activities and readings are based on themes that are relevant and interesting to adult learners such as continuing education, budgeting, community, technology, and legal problems. It can readily be used as a workbook for one-to- one tutoring and/or independent study.

Peyton, Joy Kreeft (1993). *Dialogue Journals: Interactive Writing to Develop Language and Literacy.* ERIC Digest (ERIC Document Reproduction Service No. ED 354789).

This article defines dialogue journals and includes excerpts from the dialogue journal of a teacher and her ESOL student which illustrate the benefits of this technique. The logistics, frequency, length of writing instructions, and topics are discussed. ERIC documents are available by calling EDRS at 1-800-443 3742.

Raimes, A. (1978). Problems and Teaching Strategies in ESL Composition. In *Language in Education: Theories and Practice* (14). Arlington, VA: Center for Applied Linguistics (ERIC Document Reproduction Service No. ED 175243).

This article provides a systematic discussion of the specific problems that ESOL students have composing in English. Raimes explores the probable cause of the problems and offers strategies for addressing them.

ESOL Instructional Resources for Grammar

Azar, B.S. (1984). *Basic English Grammar.* Englewood Cliffs, NJ: Prentice Hall Regents.

This is the beginning level grammar text in a series of three books by Betty Azar. The three books in the series are:

Basic English Grammar
low-and mid beginner

Fundamentals of English Grammar
    low-intermediate/intermediate

Understanding and Using English Grammar
    intermediate/advanced

The texts are presented in chapters by grammatical structures. The important grammatical points are presented in well-organized and easy-to-read charts with brief explanations and examples. The exercises in these texts practice both oral and written language. They move from exercises focused on the manipulation of meaning and form to ones that demand more independent usage and a combination of skills. All three texts are accompanied by workbooks with self-study and guided-study exercises. Teacher's guides also accompany each level and contain suggestions as well as answer keys.

Diolata, E. (1997). *Take Charge! A Student-Centered Approach to English*. New York: McGraw-Hill.

This series has two levels. Book 1 is for adult learners who have low literacy in their native language and Book 2 is for more advanced beginners who have some English skills and a solid native language literacy background. Each level has a grammar workbook which can be used with or without the student text. The grammar workbook gives simple explanations of grammar items that appear in the corresponding student text and provides several practice exercises for each grammar point.

Murphy, R. (1995). *Basic Grammar in Use: Reference and Practice for Students of English*. New York: Cambridge University Press.

This textbook focuses on the fundamental structures of English grammar taught in basic or introductory courses. It is useful as a reference on basic grammar structures for the teacher as well as a text for the beginning-level student. New structures with examples are introduced on the left-hand page and corresponding practice exercises appear on the right-hand page. This text offers precise grammar explanations in clear and simple language. There is also an answer key to the exercises.

Murphy, R. and Altman, R.. (1995). *Grammar in Use: Reference and Practice for Intermediate Students of English*. New York: Cambridge University Press.

This textbook is a reference and practice book for the intermediate learner of English. It concentrates on structures that cause much difficulty for intermediate students, such as tense, modals, conditionals, if-clauses, and prepositions. The format follows Basic Grammar in Use, where the grammar structure is introduced with examples on the left-hand side and practice exercises are given on the right-hand side. The appendices list present and past tenses, regular and irregular verbs, spelling, and short forms. There is also an answer key to the exercises which can accompany the text.

Werner, P. K., Nelson, J. P., and Spaventa, M. (1997). *Interactions Access: A Communicative Grammar*. Second edition. New York: McGraw-Hill.

This is a beginning-level grammar text for students who can understand and produce a minimal amount of conversational English. Students should at least be able to handle basic courtesy and travel situations. They should also be capable of producing simple written statements and write limited, practical English, but at only a basic, elementary level. It can be accompanied by the Interactions Access Reading/Writing Book and the Interactions Access Listening/Speaking Book. These three Interactions Access books make up the first level in a five-part series. The five levels are as follows:

Interactions Access
   Beginning to High-Beginning

Interactions One
   High-Beginning to Low-Intermediate

Interactions Two
   Low-Intermediate to Intermediate

Mosaic One
   Intermediate to High-Intermediate

Mosaic Two
   High-Intermediate to Advanced

Interactions provides a *Communicative Grammar Book* while *Mosaic* provides a *Content-Based Grammar Book.* Both *Interactions* and *Mosaic* supplement the grammar books with books concentrating on reading, writing, listening, and speaking.

ESOL Instructional Resources for Vocabulary

Collis, H. (1997). *101 American English Idioms: Understanding and Speaking Like an American.* Passport Books: Lincoln-wood, IL.

This book arranges everyday idioms into nine lighthearted sections. Each idiom has a standard English "translation" and is placed in a real-life context to facilitate understanding and to make the idioms come alive.

McCarthy, M., O'Dell, F., and Shaw, G. (1997). *Vocabulary in Use: Upper Intermediate Self Study Reference and Practice for Students of North American English.* New York: Cambridge University Press.

This vocabulary text is intended for high intermediate to advanced learners to expand their knowledge of English vocabulary. It introduces approximately 3,000 new vocabulary words in an easy-to-use format which presents vocabulary on the left-hand page and innovative practice activities on the right-hand page. A complete answer key is included, along with an index of phonetic transcriptions.

Molinsky, S. J. and Bliss, B. (1995). *Word by Word Picture Dictionary.* Englewood Cliffs, NJ: Prentice Hall Regents.

This is a picture dictionary that presents over 3,000 words in lively full-color contextualized illustrations. The vocabulary words are introduced through 97 different topics such as personal information, everyday activities, clothing, sports, etc. A unique conversational approach gives students communication practice with every word on every page. Supplements include *Workbooks: Literacy, Beginning,*

& Intermediate, Handbook of Vocabulary Teaching Strategies, and a *Teacher's Resource Book* and *Activity Masters.* The latter suggests activities for teaching the vocabulary given in the dictionary and provides detailed language and culture notes and reproducible masters.

Parnwell, E.C. (1988). *The New Oxford Picture Dictionary.* New York: Oxford University Press.

This dictionary presents over 2,400 vocabulary words, clearly depicted in contextualized illustrations. Vocabulary is grouped into 92 different topics which range from such basic subject matter as food, clothing, and shelter to such topics as sports, animals, and occupations. At the end of the dictionary is an index with a pronunciation guide. Supplements include *Beginner's* and *Intermediate Workbooks* for vocabulary exercises, which follow the format of the dictionary and a *Teacher's Guide* for beginning through advanced level students, which offers introductory language and culture notes as well as suggestions for activities and other ways to use the picture dictionary.

Proctor, P., ed. (1997). *Cambridge International Dictionary of English.* New York: Cambridge University Press.

This dictionary presents approximately 100,000 entries arranged alphabetically under 50,000 head words. The different meanings of a word are separated into different entries which are clearly indicated by guide words. Examples are labeled with clear, easy-to-understand codes that demonstrate all the important grammatical patterns of each word. This dictionary also defines thousands of common English sayings and idioms, giving learners a clear insight into the complex and culturally loaded aspects of the language.

Spears, R. A. (1995). *NTC's Dictionary of American English Phrases.* Lincoln-wood, IL: National Textbook Company.

This is a collection of frequently used phrases in American English. It contains more than 15,000 complete sentence examples for approximately 7,000 common and useful phrases. These phrases include idioms, clichés, phrasal verbs, proverbs, greetings, and good-byes. This dictionary presents in alphabetical order the core phrases that are frequently used in daily conversation and writing.

ESOL Instructional Materials for Cross-Cultural Information and Materials on U.S. Culture

Datesman, M., Crandall, J.A., and Kearny, E. (1997). *American Ways.* Second edition. Upper Saddle River, NJ: Prentice Hall.

This book explores multicultural as well as cross-cultural issues in the United States. Basic American values as well as the origin of those values are explored. The book is user-friendly with charts and diagrams that aid visual learning. Exercises include cloze, observations and interviews, and questions for discussion. This is a good source for activities to encourage interaction and conversation.

Garcia, J., Harley, S., and Howard, J. (1995). *One Nation, Many People. Volume 2. The United States Since 1876.* Paramus, NJ: Globe Fearon.

This book includes a recent history of the United States. The print is large and the vocabulary is basic. Events are broken into short paragraphs with accompanying maps, charts, and tables. Key ideas and words are highlighted.

Genzel, R.B and Graves C. M. (1994). *Culturally Speaking.* 2nd Edition. Boston: Heinle & Heinle.

This book explores cultural misunderstandings in a playful, exploratory nature. Some serious topics such as AIDS, health, and exercise are also included. There is a large section devoted to gestures. Cultural comparisons within one's own culture are explored as well. Activities include matching idioms, role plays, quizzes, and discussions.

Levine, D.R., Baxter, J., and McNulty, P. (1987). *The Culture Puzzle.* Englewood Cliffs, NJ: Prentice Hall.

This book aims to give students the skills necessary to understand the differences in communication styles across cultures and to avoid misinterpretation. Follow-up exercises include scenarios of cross-cultural differences that can be used for discussion. It is geared toward intermediate and advanced students. Language and culture are taught systematically and simultaneously.

Vogel Z. V. (1993). *Face to Face: Communication, Culture, and Collaboration.* Second edition. Boston: Heinle & Heinle.

Each chapter explores one cultural topic (work, family, school, etc.). Throughout the book are case studies based on the experiences of native speakers. The book includes many activities which are especially good for pair work.

INDEX

Nash, Andrea, 135
National Geographic, 17, 140
Native languages. See Languages
Naturalization, 197-198
Negative statements, 78, 79
Neighborhood maps, 125-126
New Lives in the New World (Magidoff), 67
New Oxford Picture Dictionary, 165, 166
New York State Department of Education, 9
News broadcasts, 61
Nodding, 130
Noises, 36
Nonverbal communication, 9-11, 18.
   See also Gestures
Norming, 42
Note-taking, 12, 47
Nouns, 196
Numbers, 81, 122-125, 158, 195, 202.
   See also Telephone numbers
Nursing, 6, 135-136
Nyeng (Vietnamese), 98
NYSPLACE (test), 53

Objects. See Real objects
Office apparatus, 144
One-to-one tutoring, 41, 158
Open-ended questions, 52, 63, 136, 141
Opposites, 143
Oral communication
   assessment of, 49
   defined, 36
   by educated persons, 6, 23, 26, 47
   limited mastery of, 48
   primacy of, 11-12
   on telephone, 60, 92, 122, 192
   See also Listening; Speaking
Our Oriental Heritage (Durant), 123
Over-articulation, 65

Paragraphs, 107, 114
Paraphrasing, 82, 98, 99, 141
Parent-teacher organizations, 149
Parents, 7, 24, 136, 137, 147. See also Mothers
Parties (social events), 122, 139-140
Past progressive tense, 112-113
Patience, 30
Pausing, 70-71
Peace Corps, 27
Personal identification, 118, 125, 189-190
Personal journals, 111, 138, 156
Personal problems, 30, 136.
   See also Responsibilities
Personal safety, 24. See also Emergencies
Personal word lists, 72. See also Word cards

Personal zone, 11, 18
Peruvian students, 63
Philippines, 93
Phonics, 107
Phrases, 64
Physical objects. See Real objects
Physician visits, 135
Picture books, 130
Picture stories, 136-137
Pictures, 119-121
   in bingo, 142
   in chain drills, 83
   in communication games, 147
   in completion drills, 86
   in comprehension checks, 114
   in dialogues, 88, 89, 90, 91
   in homework assignments, 154
   in Language Experience, 102
   in response drills, 76, 77
   in storytelling, 155-156
   in vocabulary development, 95
   See also Cartoons; Flashcards; Stick drawings
Pitch (intonation), 38, 65, 66-68, 72, 80
Placement tests, 130
Planning charts, 156, 158. See also Lesson plans
Plurals, 143
Polish students, 140
Population Bureau, 5
Portfolios, 52-53, 103, 164, 165
Portuguese language, 46
Positive statements, 78, 79
Potluck meals, 139-140
Prany (Laotian), 22
Prepositions, 113
Present progressive tense, 112
Prewriting, 110
Prices, 124, 195
Printing (manuscript writing),
   100-101, 108, 118, 202
Problem posing/solving, 135-136
Process writing, 110-111
Professional persons, 6, 37
Progress reports, 32, 33, 40, 52
Progressive tenses, 112-113
Pronunciation
   approaches to, 71
   assessment of, 52
   in audiolingual approach, 13
   deemphasis of, 63-64
   of numbers, 123
   of personal information, 118
   phonetic writing of, 133
   planning charts on, 156
   recordings and, 90, 141

Vargas, Juan, 22-23
Vella, Jane, 136
Verb tenses, 79, 85-86, 112-113, 129
VESOL (Vocational ESOL), 48
Vietnamese immigrants, 98, 139
    illiterate, 46
    literate, 48
    pregnant, 175
    skilled, 6, 99
Visual aids, 118. See also Maps; Pictures;
    Real objects
Vo Tuny, 48
Vocabulary, 37
    adaptation of, 55-56, 63, 94
    in audiolingual approach, 13
    in colored paper exercises, 132, 133, 134
    in completion drills, 86
    expansion of, 95-96, 113
    in Language Experience, 103, 104
    lesson plan for, 151
    for objects, 60
    sequential/balanced formula and, 97
    in substitution drills, 72, 73
Vocabulary games, 143-145
Vowels, 109-110

Warnings, 12
Weather reports, 141
Wei Li, 47
Wh- questions, 62
Women, 16, 18, 125. See also Mothers
Word cards
    pattern words on, 110
    sight words on, 105, 106
    in vocabulary development, 96, 103, 133
    See also Personal word lists
Word groupings, 95-96, 144, 153
Word order, 94
Word patterns, 109-110
Workplaces. See Jobs
Workshops, 29
World Wide Web, 17
Writing
    of backward buildup drills, 80
    of commands, 59, 60, 132, 133
    comprehension checked by, 61
    of dialogues, 91
    in journals, 111, 138, 156
    in Language Experience, 103, 110
    limited mastery of, 48
    of new words, 95

    of paraphrases, 98, 99
    of response drills, 77
    scripts for, 100-101
    secondary importance of, 11-12
    See also Literacy; Process writing

Yes/no questions, 62, 141

Zairean students, 146